Ashley Adams

Ashley Adams has been playing poker since 1963 when he learned it, literally, at his grandfather's knee. Since then he has gone on to be a winning home game and casino player, having played and won cash games and small tournaments all over the world. He is a poker author as well, having penned over 1,000 poker articles (for Card Player Magazine, Poker Player Newspaper, pokernews.com, and many other publications and websites) and two poker books: Winning 7-card Stud (Kensington 2002) and Winning No Limit Hold'em (Lighthouse 2011). He is also the host, since 2007, of the longest running broadcast poker radio show in the world, House of Cards (www.houseofcardsradio.com). He is happily married, with two poker playing daughters and now a granddaughter, whom he is eager to instruct in poker. He lives in Roslindale (a section of Boston) Massachusetts.

Great Poker Books from D+B

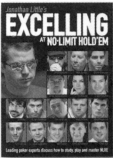
Jonathan Little's
EXCELLING
AT NO-LIMIT HOLD'EM
Leading poker experts discuss how to study, play and master NLHE

POKER BRAT
PHIL HELLMUTH'S AUTOBIOGRAPHY
THE STORY OF THE WORLD'S GREATEST POKER PLAYER
FOREWORD BY DANIEL NEGREANU

MODERN POKER THEORY
BUILDING AN UNBEATABLE STRATEGY BASED ON GTO PRINCIPLES
MICHAEL ACEVEDO
D+B

MARTIN HARRIS
POKER & Pop Culture
♠ ♥ ♣ ♦
TELLING THE STORY OF AMERICA'S FAVORITE CARD GAME

MASTERING
SMALL STAKES NO-LIMIT HOLD'EM
JONATHAN LITTLE
Strategies to consistently beat small stakes poker tournaments and cash games

ADVANCED CONCEPTS in No-Limit Hold'em
HUNTER CICHY

MASTERING MIXED GAMES
WINNING STRATEGIES FOR DRAW, STUD AND FLOP GAMES
DYLAN LINDE
FOREWORD BY PHIL HELLMUTH

FOSSILMAN'S
WINNING TOURNAMENT STRATEGIES
GREG RAYMER

Life's a Gamble
Mike Sexton
Poker Ambassador

Jonathan Little
FREE
Secrets of Professional Tournament Poker
Volume 3: The Complete Workout

THE PURSUIT OF POKER SUCCESS
LEARN FROM 50 OF THE WORLD'S BEST POKER PLAYERS
LANCE BRADLEY

THE MYTH OF POKER TALENT
EXPLOITATIVE PLAY IN LIVE POKER
Alexander Fitzgerald
How to manipulate your opponents into making mistakes

FROM VIETNAM TO VEGAS!
HOW I WON THE WORLD SERIES OF POKER MAIN EVENT
QUI NGUYEN AND STEVE BLAY
A HAND-BY-HAND ANALYSIS OF QUI'S HISTORIC VICTORY
FOREWORD BY ANTONIO ESFANDIARI

MOORMAN'S BOOK OF POKER
MOORMAN

Dr. Patricia Cardner with Gareth James
PURPOSEFUL PRACTICE FOR POKER
THE MODERN APPROACH TO STUDYING POKER

Mastering Pot-Limit Omaha
the modern aggressive approach
Herbert Okolowitz & Wladimir Taschner
D+B

WINNING POKER IN 30 MINUTES A DAY

ASHLEY ADAMS

POKER

First published in 2020 by D & B Publishing

Copyright © 2020 Ashley Adams

British Library Cataloguing-in-Publication Data
A catalogue record for this book is available from the British Library.

ISBN: 978 1 91286 212 2

All sales enquiries should be directed to D&B Publishing:
e-mail: info@dandbpoker.com; website: www.dandbpoker.com

Cover design by Horatio Monteverde.
Printed and bound by Versa Press in the US.

To Charles Fishbein, owner of the world's finest coffee store:
The Coffee Exchange of Providence Rhode Island.
He created the poker player's perfect coffee: Full House Blend.

Contents

Acknowledgments

I have a few people to thank, without whose help and support I would not have finished this excellent book.

Thank you to Tricia Cardner, who made the connection to the fine publisher D&B, and to its owners Byron Jacobs and Dan Addelman who literally made this book. A large bow of gratitude to Howard Swains, the best editor a writer could ask for.

Many thanks to the Weischadle brothers, Dave and Doug, who, in addition to being expert entertainment lawyers, produce the world's best gambling radio show *House of Cards*. Gratitude to my long-time friend Paul Sax, who in addition to saving thousands of lives as one of the foremost experts in infectious disease also manages to save me a seat every so often in his great home game.

Thank you to my brother Joshua Adams for technical support and encouragement, to my brother Lee Adams and his son Tucker, who, through their interest and enthusiasm for poker have kept my interest in the game keen even as it might have flagged. Thank you to my daughter Hannah Adams for suggesting how I might organize this material in a way that would allow me to get it done. Thank you to my friend Andrei Joseph who has been instrumental in keeping me in the poker scene even as I grew weary at times; to my friend Jim Hexter, who has accompanied me on many trips to poker games everywhere; and to David Kluchman, David Kuznick, Ming Lee, Bugsy, and all of the others who play in an excellent home poker game at an undisclosed location north of Boston, and who inspire me to be a better player.

A memorial tribute to my inspiration for poker writing, the most accomplished gambling and poker writer, Ed Silberstang. And also a serious nod of appreciation to his son, the multi-talented businessman, poker writer, novelist, father, and owner of the Gambler's General Store, Avery Cardoza.

I owe my ability to play poker without any familial restraints to my amazing wife Debi. I owe my early and continued interest in poker to my grandfather Max Levine, who first taught me the game, my father Bill Pozefsky, who patiently explained to me that there were poker games other than five-card draw, and to my mother Carol Pozefsky, who kept the light on for me as I returned from late-night poker playing sessions in high school.

But my greatest thanks of all goes to the players in America's Best Home Game, led by the amazingly generous and loyal host Jeff Green and also his compadres in poker, Dale, Hubie, Johnny, Lou, Jimmy, Larry, Wurm and a rotating cast of others who come to this great Man Cave to play Loutardo, Boston Stud, Shrewsbury Stud, Aviator, Reveal, 2-1-3, and countless other poker games we invent. You guys have helped inspire me to do this and have put up with my absence for all these months as I have written this. Thanks guys – you are what real poker is all about!

Preface

Why This Book?

Let's be clear about one thing first. This is a book about just one of the many games you might find in a public poker room: No Limit Texas Hold'em cash games. Even so, there are so many no limit hold'em poker books on the market today, why add another one?

Truly, the question crossed my mind many times before I decided to take on this project. My answer is simple. Though there are plenty of poker books aimed at the good, winning no limit hold'em player, there are few books for the typical cash game player, who breaks even or loses a bit, and who simply wants to improve his game. I don't think there's a really good book that addresses the typical poker player who wants to stop losing and start winning in a public poker room.

I'm not talking about the rank beginner. There are plenty of books for them – teaching the rank of the hands, the origins of the game, and how to play. But I don't think the typical player needs to learn the rudiments of the game. They're already playing poker. But they are intimidated by a lot of the highly technical material out there today and may not want to commit the kind of time and energy it appears to take to get really good.

This book looks to turn losing, break-even, beginning and intermediate players into winning players. It presumes you know something of the game – and have played it. But it also presumes that either you don't feel confident playing in a public poker room or that you don't seem to be consistently beating the game.

If you read this book and do the simple exercises I provide, I am confident that you will learn the way to win. You might not win very much at first. You will not be an expert capable of taking on the toughest players in the biggest games. But you will have the skills to defeat the typically bad and mediocre players you face in home games, house games, and public poker room games. You will also know how to spot the kind of players from whom you can win money.

The book is organized into broad chapters and short sections. Many of those sections have simple exercises at the end of them. You need to do the exercises. It will never take you more than 30 minutes to complete them. But you'll need to do them to make sure you've mastered the material. It's simple material to be sure. But it takes at least some reflection and practice to get a full handle on it.

I recommend that throughout the process you keep a poker notebook. Write down your experiences, your thoughts, and your questions. When you're done with the book, look back over the questions you asked. I suspect you'll know the answers to many of them once you're done.

I want you to learn the tools you'll need to beat the typical entry level, or slightly above entry level no limit hold'em game found in public poker rooms today. Specifically, that would be $1/2 and $1/3 games. Toward that end, you'll need to focus first on three very broad missions: find games that you can beat; beat those games with a simple, very tight and aggressive strategy; and learn the techniques for beating tougher players in tougher games.

When we are done, if you stay with this from start to finish, you will have all the tools you need to crush the $1/2 and $1/3 no limit cash games that are popular today. With good practice and self-control, you should become a consistent winner.

Ashley Adams, January 2020

Chapter One

Game Selection:
Before You Even Sit Down

In this chapter we will look at the ever-important subjects of game selection and seat selection. All games are not created equal, as I'll show you. Similarly, the seat you're in will often determine how well you're likely to do. While it's true that not everyone has the luxury of many games to choose from, learning these game and seat selection skills will help you, at least to some extent, even if your choices are quite limited.

What you'll learn
How to know whether a game and a seat are likely to be profitable, and how to adjust your game strategy to make the best of the table and seat you're in.

Why it's important
Your profit comes entirely from other players. You need to make sure you are in the right position to take advantage of bad and mediocre players.

Introduction

I want you to imagine that you are learning to ski. You're not going to start on the black diamond course with a narrow path running steeply and dangerously downhill between trees. While that would surely be exciting, it might also prove deadly, given your limited skills.

Instead, when you're learning to ski, you typically start on a big wide hill. No turns. No trees. There's a good deal of distance on either side of you as you descend the slope. It's just a simple, plain hill. You start here because you want to work on your basic technique without risk to life or limb.

You learn to ski without falling. And you learn how to fall safely. You learn first how to limit your speed by going downhill in a snowplow position and then you gradually and safely learn how to turn. It's a simple, incremental approach to skiing that emphasizes safety first.

I'd like to do the same thing with your poker game. While you *might* become a great player by jumping in with excellent players right off the bat, it might also result in the fatal demise of your bankroll. Rather, I'd like to teach you how to play incrementally, with a safe and sound basic strategy. You'll learn a method of play that will be boring and simple at first, with very little room for discretion on your part. There will be little twisting or turning (though there will be some). You will be moving moderately, though steadily, with little excitement and only modest risk.

In poker parlance, you will learn to play extremely tightly – playing only a few, high-value starting hands. You will play these hands with little or no deception. You will tend to play these few hands aggressively – saying to all who listen that you have a very strong hand to start with – and that they should stay out of your way. This approach would not be very effective against the best players. They would soon figure you out and it would be like playing your cards face-up against them. But, if you follow good game selection, you will have opponents who will either not hear or not care about this loud message (and the strongest players will generally just avoid you when you are in a pot). The weak players will play against you even though you are shouting "Strong hand!" They will lose money to you in the process.

Your profit will come not from fooling your better opponents, but by crushing the bad ones with hands that are typically stronger than theirs. In that sense, your advantage will come from their willingness to play against you, in spite of the fact that you will be obviously playing your best hand strongly, and your drawing hands carefully, and only for the right odds. Your ideal opponents will be those who do not have the knowledge or self-control to stay out of your way. So your first objective will be to find games with those types of players. Our first lesson will therefore be in game selection.

Where Your Profit Comes From

Game Selection

All poker games are different. Some games will be extremely profitable; others will be so tough that you are almost assured of losing money, especially when considering the rake. Your job is to find the game that is the most likely to be profitable for you – and to avoid the games where you will be playing against better players. In short, you will be hunting for the best game.

Doing so is a skill that is at least as important as learning how to play well. That's why we're covering it first, even before covering a basic strategy of play.

Your profit will come from the difference between your skill and the average skill of your opponents. Of course it won't accrue to you in every hand you play. You will win some pots, and lose some pots no matter how good the game and how bad your opponents. All the while, your chip stack will fluctuate. You will have to have the intestinal fortitude to continue to play even after you lose money, and to stay in the game even when you are ahead and may want to leave with a small profit. When you are ahead you'll have to restrain your eagerness to play more loosely just because you have won a hand and might be temporarily ahead of the game. And when you are behind you'll have to inhibit the natural tendency to tighten up or leave to stop any more losses – or to bet it all in one last desperate attempt to get back to even.

Since your profit will come from the disparity between how you apply your overall skill as a poker player and the average skill of your opponents, you are going to look for games with opponents with little skill. You are also going to look for specific opponents from whom you will be better able to win money.

By "skill" I don't mean just their knowledge of poker. I mean their ability to consistently play well. Appearances in that regard are sometimes deceiving, by the way. It's important to look beyond the surface when figuring out whether the game is good. Just because someone knows a lot of poker terminology and lingo, or acts quickly at the table, or deftly tosses in their chips, or hob nobs with dealers and other players, that doesn't mean that they have any real poker skill. What you're looking for are players who are more likely to lose their money to you. In that regard there are some very specific and simple things to look for. You shouldn't get distracted by the superficial traits that are largely irrelevant.

As you progress through the chapter below, and see how to determine if a game and a seat will be profitable, I recognize that players are often seated into certain games and seats regardless of the player's initial preferences. The brush or floor person may often just brings you to a seat at a table without asking you where you'd prefer to play. Even so, you must exercise your ability to change tables as seats become available, always considering where you would ideally like to be seated. Doing so should be part of your playing arsenal.

The Seven Signs of a Good Game

There are dozens, perhaps hundreds, of small signs that a game is likely to be profitable for you. I'd like to start with just seven big ones.

1) Sufficient Money on the Table

You can't profit at poker if your opponents have little or no money for you to win. That is easy to size up in casino poker as the games are played "table stakes". "Table stakes" means that for the duration of each hand, you are playing only for the money that is on the table in front of you. Players are forbidden from going into their pockets for more money while a hand is in play. Nor may they take money off the table (known colloquially as "rabbit holing") until they are ready to completely leave the game.

Accordingly, one obvious indicator of whether the game may be good is whether there are a lot of big stacks of poker chips in front of players on the table. While seeing big stacks doesn't necessarily mean the game is good, seeing only short stacks is a clear sign that you should avoid the game.

What's a short stack? It depends on the game. A $200 stack in front of a player in a $1/2 no limit game is a good-sized stack. But $200 in a $5/10 no limit game is very short. Generally, you want players to have, on average, no less than 75 to 100 times the big blind. So in a $1/2 game you'd like to see at least a few stacks greater than $200 and no less than a total of $1,000 on a full table. In a $5/10 game you want players with $750 or more in front of them (but when you are beginning you will tend to avoid games above $1/3 since they are not likely to have a lot of the right type of soft opponents for you to play against).

For the sake of simplicity, unless indicated otherwise, I am assuming a $1/2 no limit game (meaning the small blind is $1 and the big blind is $2), with a minimum $60 buy-in and a maximum $300 buy-in.

An indication of a bad game is the prevalence of low denomination chips. In the $1/2 game, for example, you want to avoid no limit games with a lot of $1 chips (usually white). These games will usually play especially tightly, when compared with games where the standard chip is a $5 chip. There will typically be much smaller pots than even small *limit* hold'em games.

Case in point. I played in a Sacramento, California card room with two games: $2-$4 limit poker and $1/2 no limit poker. Typically, the no limit game plays much bigger than the limit game. But in this casino, the $2-$4 game was clearly the bigger of the two games, with much more money typically at risk. This was because, among other reasons, players in the no limit game used only $1 chips and started with $20 or $40 stacks, all in white. They would either fold to the big blind or call. Thereafter bets would be $2, $3 or $4, with little raising. Pots would be in the $10 or

$12 range. The 10% $4 rake was taken right out of the blinds in $1 increments, with $3 swept out no matter what the size of the initial pre-flop pot. Players would typically win a pot of $8 or so, of which $2 or more was their own money. It was a terrible game.

The $2-4 game, by contrast, was a much wilder affair. It was played with $2 chips, with two $2 blinds. Players frequently raised and re-raised pre-flop, building the pot. The flop was almost always bet, with players wildly raising. Given the size of the pot, and the great pot odds players were getting, almost everyone eventually called, further engorging the pot. Typically, there would be a $4 bet on the turn, often a few raises, and incredibly loose calls. Then the multi-way river would be bet, with typically at least a few people calling to keep the bettors and raisers honest. Pots were often in the $100 to $140 range. The rake was still tough to beat. But since it was capped at $4, it would end up being no more than 4% or so of the pot. Given the multi-way nature of the game, this ended up being no more than 5-6% of a player's winnings, as opposed to a rake that frequently took 20% of a player's winning in the no limit game.

In addition to average chip stacks and the denomination of the chips in play, you want to look at individual stack sizes. Ideally, there will be at least a player or two with a stack that is at least 200 times the size of the big blind. You want the opportunity to double up a couple of times through an especially deep player.

It's not sufficient for these players to have big stacks. You also want those deep players to be engaged in regular action – not protecting their stacks with little or no play. It's not infrequent to see a no limit game with a bunch of short stacks and one huge stack. This is often an indicator that the big-stacked guy has stacked a few opponents at different stages of the game. Sometimes it's because he is a very aggressive player who is still playing aggressively – frequently putting his opponents to the test by raising them. That's what you'd like to see: having this deep-stacked player regularly putting his chips at risk by playing many hands, and playing them aggressively. Sometimes, however, you will arrive at the game at a time when this player has decided, for whatever reason, to protect that stack. This is often the case late at night and early in the morning, when he's tired or bored, or just weary. So don't assume that just because there's a large stack or two that they are engaged in action. Watch the game for a while to determine how active the deep-stacked players really are. You want them in many of the hands.

2) Looseness

Your assessment of profitability should also include observing how loose it is playing. You generally want to see more than two competitors fighting it out for the pot. The ideal game is one with at least three players showing down their hands at the river. You want multi-way action if possible – an indicator that at least one of the competitors in the hand is playing loosely. In general, the more players who stay in to see the flop the better. And the longer they stay in the hand the better. Yes, it's true that if everyone calls everything, you won't be able to manipulate people out of the pot. Yes, it's true that with lots of opponents, your best starting hands will not win as often as if you are only up against a lone opponent. That's okay. In fact it's usually what you want. Over time, you will do better with many loose opponents than with a bunch of tight opponents who fold all the time. So look for multi-way pots.

You will sometimes hear the refrain, "That game is too loose to beat" or words to that effect. Don't listen. That is wrong. While it can be frustrating to lose many hands in a row to players who call pre-flop and on the flop with much the worst of it and then get lucky on the turn and river, if you play a more skillful game than these extremely loose opponents, you can and will win their money in the long run. It is a mathematical certainty.

3) Passive Play

You want to see players who check and call rather than bet and raise. There are many reasons this is a good thing for you. Most important, it will give you an opportunity to see your drawing hands develop cheaply, allowing you to profitably play a wider range of hands that can develop into winners. You want to be in the position to decide when and how you play your hands. You can best do that with opponents who don't tend to play aggressively.

You want to avoid games that pressure you to make tough decisions about whether to continue to play or to fold especially when you are starting out. Eventually, you will be comfortable against any type of opponent. But when you are first learning to play competitively, the less betting pressure on you from your opponents the better.

4) Happy, Gambling Opponents

You are going to be serious about your play because your goal is to win money. But you don't want your opponents to be as serious as you. You'd like them to be there to have a good time, there to gamble or for the social experience. You want players who will gladly go up against you even when you are betting aggressively with your strong hands.

The great thing about poker is that it can be both a game of skill and a game of luck *at the same time*! Accordingly, you want opponents who view poker as a fun game of luck, while you are playing it as a game of skill. You want to see the signs that they are not too serious.

One sign that they are not taking the game too seriously is their general disposition. Do they look serious? Are they frowning, concentrating, sitting with their arms folded in front of them, leaning back, and generally focused on the task at hand? When the flop hits, are they staring at you, to get a read on your reaction to the flop, rather than staring at the flop itself? If so, that's not likely to be good for you. On the other hand, are they laughing, lighthearted, talking easily to each other? That *is* generally good for you. Gravitate toward that kind of atmosphere.

5) Signs of Other Forms of Gambling

A game is also inviting if you see physical signs of other forms of gambling. Are there players filling out keno forms, for example? (Keno is a casino gambling game with very bad odds for the players.) Are they playing the horses? Are they betting on sports while they play? Are they distracted by watching sporting events? I'm not suggesting that sports bettors and horseplayers can't be good poker players. They surely can be. But if they're gambling on other things, it's likely that they view poker as largely a gamble too, and may be softer opponents than those who are grinding it out, focused on the game.

6) Drinking Alcohol

Booze is a great indicator that there may be some soft opponents you'd like to play against. Look around at the cup holders. If they hold beer, mixed drinks, or wine, be encouraged. For the most part, drinkers are not serious poker players. They are there to have a good time. If, on the other hand, the only things you see are water bottles and cups of coffee, be alert that these might be serious players.

Seeing other players drinking is good for two main reasons. First of all, alcohol has a positive effect (for you) on an opponent's play. Alcohol tends to diminish inhibition and self control, so players will tend to play more loosely, carelessly, and recklessly. It's also good because it indicates a player who is not playing chiefly to win money. Serious players tend to avoid alcohol, so seeing it tends to indicate that the player is not serious. That's what you want. An ideal game is one in which people aren't serious about winning money.

Two words of caution are in order. Firstly, there are many good players (and some great ones) who play perfectly well while drinking. Make sure that you don't underestimate a player's abilities just because he's drinking. Another concern is that while drinking is usually good for the game, having a drunk at the table can be bad – for a couple of reasons. Though drunk play is almost always terrible play, it is also usually very slow play. This can be frustrating. It can also hurt your bottom line by greatly diminishing the number of hands an hour you will play. To the extent that it sets off other players – causing them to play poorly and impatiently, it's a good thing. But you have to be very careful that it doesn't set you off in the same way, sabotaging your best play even as you hungrily eye the drunk's chips.

7) Predictable, Tight and Timid Opponents at the Table

While loose, passive opponents are ideal for a good game, a line-up of predictable, tight and timid opponents can also be very useful. This is especially true if you don't have a high rake chewing up the small pots.

Players sometimes get into a zone – a tired habitual zone that can affect the entire table. This is often the case in the wee hours of the morning in a 24-hour room, when players are engaged in a long session. They are frequently playing on auto-pilot, trying perhaps to "just get back to even" as they wait for a monster hand, or a monster flop. These games are profitable because you can inflate and then steal many pots as you use aggression against opponents who will predictably fold if they don't hit their hands on the flop. (Statistically, they usually won't.) This is especially the case when there is a high hand or bad beat promotion. Many players are in the game chiefly to try and hit the jackpot. They will play hands that have some promise of becoming the monsters they need to qualify for the promotion but then immediately get away from them when it's clear they can no longer win. Their goal is just to stay in for the flop.

For example, if there's a promotion paying out $500 to the high hand of the hour, these "high hand whores", as they are familiarly known, will play 7♦-4♦ even for a raise pre-flop hoping to hit the extremely long-shot straight flush that will earn the bonus. But then when the flop appears, and hitting a straight flush is no longer possible, they will fold to a bet.

These are ideal opponents if you are alert and ready to take advantage of them. Look for games with players in this kind of mood. Build the pots early and then steal them after the flop or on the turn.

Scouting For a Good Game

Your first two exercises are going to involve a field trip to the largest poker room in the area to apply what you've learned about game selection. You may use these exercises to find a game in which you will play. You may elect to just go and observe. But whether you play or not, you will apply your powers of observation to determine whether the games are likely to be profitable.

Exercise 1

Check stack size, looseness, fun, and drinking in the game.

1) Determine Average Stack Size

Add up the stack sizes of the players in each game. Do this in your head. You'd like to be inconspicuous if you can. Calculate the average chip stack by dividing the total size of the stacks by the number of players.

Determine whether the average stack is at least 100 times the big blind. That is easy. If it's a $1/2 no limit game, 100 x $2 is $200. So you want to see if the average stack is at least $200. Also take note of any games with especially large stacks. Ideally you'd like to see at least one stack of $400 in a $1/2 game, $600 in a $1/3 game and $1,500 in a $2/5 game.

Watch those players with the big stacks for a few hands. Observe specifically whether the largest stacks are regularly engaged in the game or whether they seem to be playing very tightly. Then rank the games in order of how profitable they may be, without regard to the skill level of the players in the game.

2) Determine the Looseness of the Game

You want to make an assessment of how loosely the game plays to decide whether the game is profitable for you. Simply add up the number of players who see the flop, then the number who see the turn, and then the number who see the river. Add the three streets together and then divide by three. Anything under three is tight. Anything more than four is loose. Observe at least five hands per table.

3) Assess How Much Fun Players Are Having

On the one hand this is silly. How can you assess "fun"? On the other hand, players who are having a good time are more likely to be the loose, happy-go-lucky opponents that you want to face. So, as you observe the average chip stack and the looseness of the game, make a mental note of how much fun the players seem to be having, and how much non-poker gambling they seem to be doing. This is admittedly highly subjective.

Nevertheless, do the best you can. Give the game a number from 1 to 5 with 1 being the worst – dour, sour, serious, somber players – and 5 being the best – laughing, drinking, fun-loving gamblers.

4) Observe How Much Drinking is Going on
Look around the table and literally count how many players appear to have an alcoholic beverage in front of them. Three or more is ideal.

Exercise 2

Review All Seven Signs of a Good Game
Make a quick list of all of the lower buy-in no limit hold'em games ($1/2, $1/3, and $2/5). Observe them each for at least two or three hands. As you observe the games, see if any of them fall into any of the seven categories of good games listed above. If they do, make a note of which categories they fall into and then review your list. Circle the one or two games that you think would be most profitable.

Keeping the Game Good: Your Own Behavior

You want to behave in a manner at the poker table that encourages your opponents to have a good time. Much as an advantage blackjack player doesn't want the house to know he is counting cards, neither do you want your opponents to view you as a particularly serious, skill-based, strategy-driven player. True, they may tend to figure that out as you generally succeed in winning their money. But you don't want to accelerate their education with the way you behave. And you certainly don't want to piss them off by behaving arrogantly or obnoxiously.

Toward this end, it is helpful for you to project a relaxed levity. While you are in between hands, if you can, engage in friendly, though not intrusive, conversation with those who are willing to talk. You don't want to be annoying with too much chatter, and you want to be a friendly person. If others seem to be eager to chat, be a ready audience for them and their stories (especially their bad beat stories).

And yes, this means do not wear headphones or sunglasses. They inhibit the type of friendly player you want to be.

Similarly, feel free to go along with whatever mindless *low cost* betting and side-betting schemes they recommend. If, for example, one of them suggests a $4 button straddle, or proposes everyone plays a round blind before the flop, or offers a side bet of $1 a hand on whether the flop will be majority red or black, you don't have to encourage them, but don't be the one stickler at the table who refuses to partake. (If you can laugh it off and not participate that's fine.)

I'm not saying you must always engage in every ridiculous proposition that comes along. And if the proposition is expensive relative to the stakes of the game, by all means take a pass. (Don't agree to everyone shoving blind, for example.) But don't be too quick to be the one serious player and party-pooper, so long as the mindless gambling is for short money. If it is fun, and your participation will add to the levity, join in with a smile.

You want to behave at the table in a way that encourages others to willingly lose their money to you. Don't adopt the demeanor of a tough, serious, out-for-blood competitor.

This makes poker different from other competitive endeavors. When you play a sport of pure skill like baseball, football, chess, or golf, you typically want to adopt a serious no-nonsense approach to the competition. You put on your "game face". You may even try to look intimidating — frightening your opponents as you get ready to beat them.

This is not the approach to take at the poker table. Though you surely want to be highly competitive and serious about winning, you want to affect the attitude of someone who is out to have a good time. You do this to encourage that attitude in your opponents. It is that attitude that will help you win money.

The more fun your opponents are having, the more they'll feel good about losing their money to you. Of course they're not going to prefer losing to winning. But laughing and having a good time softens the blow and relaxes the inhibitions. Your job, in addition to playing your best game, is to help make the game fun for those who are losing.

I'm going to give you some specific things to avoid and to do. But I really don't need to, do I? You know what makes someone comfortable at the table, and what drives them away. You would probably make the same list of things you don't like in others and what you enjoy.

Firstly, don't point out the errors of your opponents. You're not there as a coach or instructor. If someone calls with garbage and then catches the perfect river card, don't say, sarcastically or otherwise, "Nice catch". It's only going to risk pissing them off. Don't berate them for their bad behavior. Smile, accept it and move on.

Don't whine. No one likes to hear it. Don't tell bad beat stories (though gladly listen to them). They're boring and irrelevant. Don't tell us how many hands you've lost in a row or how many times you've had aces cracked.

Here are some things you *should* do.

Tell a short funny story. People like stories — as long as you're not blabbing all the time. Joke about yourself. Self-deprecating humor never offended anyone. Don't have anything funny, silly, or self-deprecating to add? That's okay too. No one ever got pissed off because you didn't talk enough.

When there's a dispute, *you* be the one to offer to resolve it. Have a disagreement; *you* give in (if it's not expensive to do so). Someone miss a blind or an ante but nobody knows who shorted the pot, *you* put it in graciously and with a laugh. In short, you should try to be the most generous, nicest person at the table.

Exercise 3

Appropriate Behavior
Answer these questions about behavior at the table, considering whether you think it would add to or subtract from your bottom line in the long run.

1) Opponents in the $1/2 game are very loose and crazy. They are talking about playing a round with a third blind for $4. The dealer says it has to be unanimous. Do you agree with everyone else at the table to change to this structure?

2) Three players say that they are in favor of having everyone put up a $50 blind bet pre-flop in this $1/2 no limit game. In or out?

3) The guy to your right is the small blind. It's folded around to him. He asks if you chop (you each take back your blinds)? Two guys have done this already. Should you insist on playing it out without chopping, or should you agree to chop?

4) The guy to your left offers you a prop bet. He'll take $1 on the flop being red. Is that okay with you?

5) Someone proposes that each of you take a non-face card. Over the next 10 hands they'll keep track of which card comes up the most. $5 from everyone to the winner. You in or out?

6) Every single player is drinking beer, wine, or a mixed drink. You're drinking water. A player razzes you about being the only non-drinker. You're not an alcoholic. Should you order a beer?

7) You're playing $1/2. A total fish offers to bet you $5 on the heavyweight UFC fight that starts in about an hour. You know nothing about the fighters. Do you take the bet?

8) You have $1,000. You hit the nut flush on the river. Your opponent, acting first, takes his rack of $500 in chips and shoves it into the pot. You instantly call. He pulls back his rack and says he folds. The dealer is about to let him pull back his money. Do you call the floor – knowing that he'll think you a jerk?

Answers to Exercise 3

1) Yes. It's not a skillful play but it's cheap and relatively harmless.

2) Out. It's too expensive.

3) Chop. It's customary. Refusing to do so will indicate that you are extremely serious, something you don't want to reveal.

4) Yes. It's cheap fun.

5) In again. It's cheap and harmless and keeps the game fun.

6) Sure. You don't have to drink much of it, but you want to avoid attention as the only serious player at the table.

7) Yes. Five bucks is a small price to pay to play along with a guy you want to keep happy.

8) Call the floor and don't worry about being considered a jerk. Five hundred dollars is a lot of money.

Exercise 4

Write down five things you can do at the table to keep or make a game good. Now write down five things that you can do that might be technically correct but that would hurt the game.

Looking For Specific Bad Players to Exploit

You've learned how to spot a good game, but you also want to identify specific types of players who are profitable to play against. Much of the time, your profit will come from a particularly profitable hand, or a small number of hands. You'll be playing for many hours, playing carefully, waiting for and creating profitable opportunities. But you often won't be seeing a steady increase in your stack – even if the game itself is good. Instead, you'll make your money on one or a few big pots, by winning the stack of a player who has made a large mistake.

A Video Poker Analogy

In an ideal world, you want the game to be populated with at least one, and maybe even more, of those specific players from whom you can win a stack. And you want them to have enough chips for their big mistakes to be profitable for you.

In this regard, playing against bad, overly loose opponents is like playing a 101% payout video poker machine. In video poker, every once in a while, there are machines that pay out a tiny fraction more than they take in. This could be as a promotion (as a loss leader), or it's sometimes the product of a progressive jackpot feature that creates situations where the jackpot becomes large enough that the machine becomes what's known as +EV – ie, it has a positive expected value, This means that a player playing perfect strategy will have a positive expectation. Expert video poker players look for these machines.

But here's the thing: The vast majority of the time even the best players are playing at a *disadvantage*. They will be steadily, if slowly, losing money. But they do this knowing that sooner or later they will hit that jackpot. And when they do, a single large jackpot will more than compensate them for all the money they have lost the other 99.9% of the time. They just have to have the patience, the bankroll, and the correct strategy to withstand the long dry spell at the +EV video poker machine when they are slowly losing money. They also have to play perfectly the rest of the time so they *only* lose the minimum the other 99.9% of the time when they don't hit the jackpot. And of course they have to be astute enough to ferret out that one +EV machine from a sea of machines that pay less than 100%.

A good poker player, in these relatively small stakes no limit games, must often follow a similar arc toward profitability. You must first spot that +EV game. You must then have the self-control and skill to apply a strategy with which you will lose the minimum on the marginal hands while patiently waiting for the hands that will win you a very large pot, typically played against the large donors at the table. Though most of the time you may be breaking even or even losing a small amount because of the rake, a good game will be profitable because of those infrequent hands that reward you with a very large pot – sometimes in the form of another player's entire stack. This single large pot compensates you for the long periods of no pots. It means that you should be looking for very specific opponents who will pay you off if the right situation arises.

Profitable Opposing Player Profiles

We will eventually review all kinds of players and how to adjust your play to exploit them. But for starters, we want to look for a few player types that are especially prone to big losses.

You want to play against someone who has at least a fairly big stack, who can be manipulated into situations when he will be separated from it all. These players have some blend of the following characteristics.

Cluelessness

You will not often see a truly clueless opponent with a decent stack. Typically, a truly bad player, who may just be learning the game, starts out with a short stack, not wanting to get hurt too badly as they put their foot in the water. Their attitude may be that they'll bring a fixed small amount of money to gamble with – money they're prepared to lose. That amount is typically just about the table minimum - $60 to $100 in the typical $1/2 no limit game. They generally do exactly what they are prepared to do: lose their stack. But sometimes, for whatever reason, these same clueless players have a fairly large stack. Maybe they figured they had to buy in for the maximum. Maybe they are especially well-heeled, so the stakes are not a significant amount of money to them. Maybe, though they're clueless, they incorrectly assess themselves ready to play poker, and don't want to be caught short. Maybe they've been extremely lucky and have doubled up once or twice.

One scenario that I've learned to look for along these lines is a bachelor or bachelorette party – some celebration of young drinking people – standing around their friend as he or she plays poker. The friend doesn't want to disappoint the crowd, so they buy in big to impress.

No matter. If you see a clueless player with a large stack, for whatever reason, you want to pounce quickly, before someone else sits down.

Inebriated Players

You want a big-stacked inebriant for it to be worth your time – not falling down drunk necessarily – but clearly impaired. Sometimes they will come to the table with a few high denomination chips from another game like blackjack or craps. You can sometimes see them walking (or staggering) over. Follow them in if you can.

Loud, Flashy Players

Some players are looking for and creating action. True, it's sometimes an act by the extremely skilled. More often, in this game, it's real. They crave action, live for it, and play poker in a manner that has it. They will raise blind, frequently bet or raise many times the size of the pot. "$20? Make it $100!" This may be accompanied by drinking, but it need not be. You can sometimes inconspicuously double up against these gamblers, if you can hit a really strong hand. Look for them. They present a golden opportunity.

Sticky Nits

These players have learned one lesson – and learned it too well. They play very few hands, having learned to be selective in their starting cards. They are often aggressive with these hands, just as the book says. They continue to be aggressive, betting the flop and the turn. On the river they might slow down, but will almost always call your bet, convincing themselves that you are bluffing. Look for these players. They can be very profitable for you. They will pay you off when you hit two pair or better, not wanting to back away from one of the very few hands they have ventured to play.

Again, much of your profit will come from just one or two hands a session, when you stack an opponent who overplayed an inferior hand. Always be on the lookout for opportunities to do that.

How Games Change

One final thought about good and bad tables. Tables change. They tend to change from one end of the spectrum to the other. Take your great table, for example. There are a bunch of loose fish who seem determined to lose their money. You spot the game and take an empty seat in it. So far so good. But watch what tends to happen. Sooner or later, those deep-stacked fish do exactly what they appear to be trying to do: they lose their money. They are replaced, much of the time at least, by someone like you who is scouting around for a good game. They are likely to be a skilled player. The other donor at the table then also goes bust. He too is replaced by a tough regular who had been drooling two tables over, waiting for a seat to open in this great game. Now the two fish are gone, replaced with sharks like you who are highly skilled. How good do you think the game is now?

It's probably going to be tough. What is likely to happen next? I'll tell you. The good observant opponents at your table, always on the lookout for a good game, will recognize that their game has gone south. They will look for a softer game. They will notice that there's a juicy game a few tables over. One of the players there will leave and one of the skilled players in your game will move over and fill it. He in turn might well be replaced by a bad player – someone who was not astute to notice or care that your game now consists of a bunch of rocks and TAGs. So now instead of a shark you have at least one guppy in your game. The pendulum swings again and eventually you might have the compliment of players that encourages good players to move in as the bad players get eaten up and leave.

The moral to this story is that though game selection is key, sometimes the way to get to a better table is not to move but to stay – and watch your own table go from bad to good.

Exercise 5

Scouting for Opponents who Will be Profitable for You
In this exercise, you are not looking at the general quality of the game but for specific players you think are likely to be profitable for you. Look around the table. Watch it for a few hands. Identify any players who seem to fit the profitable profiles above (clueless, loud/flashy, sticky nit, drunk). Make a note of their seat numbers (how many to the left of the dealer). Go from table to table until you have identified the games that have at least one player who is likely to be profitable to play against.

Other Considerations in Game Selection

The Most Profitable Time to Play

Poker rooms are often open 24 hours a day, seven days a week. Even those that close are usually open until relatively late at night. You can often pick just about any time to play. Is there an ideal time for your poker?

From my experience, you're going to find the best games late at night and often far into the early morning hours. This is especially true in casinos that serve free or inexpensive alcohol, even if they have a "last call" at some time. Before last call, many players are taking advantage of the free booze. And after last call they are often still inebriated – or exhausted. Inebriation and exhaustion are excellent lubricants for bad play.

Similarly, weekends are generally better times to play than weekdays. This is especially true if there is a hotel on site or nearby, when partying players are out for a weekend of fun. The best times are on holiday weekends when revelers have three days away from their regular lives to party and gamble it up.

Your lifestyle may not allow you the freedom of picking exactly when and how you visit a public poker room. But if you have the flexibility to decide exactly when you play, and if circumstances provide for a trip to a poker-rich environment, I would focus on the holiday weekends. You can arrive late evening on a Friday, and play as long as you can remain awake and disciplined at the table. You can then sleep until you're well rested, and repeat your playing schedule on Saturday and Sunday, leaving at checkout on Monday.

For those of you who want to play during the week, or who can't stay overnight, look to the end of the week, and look to start play after work on a Wednesday or Thursday. Again, play as late as your schedule will allow.

Just to reiterate this point: try to avoid mid-week games in the late morning and afternoon. They tend to be filled with conservative, short-stacked retirees, more interested in nursing their small buy-in and waiting for a high hand or bad beat than they are in gambling it up with you. That's a huge generalization, and there are always exceptions, but it holds as a rule of thumb. (I know of one professional in a California room who spent a dozen years feasting off of wealthy retirees who all arrived at 10:00 a.m. and left for dinner at 6 p.m. I know of a poker room that has it's best game on Monday evening, starting at 6:00 p.m., when area guys in cash businesses show up with tons of gamble and tons of cash. If you find such a group, terrific! Go when there's great action, at any time of day that you can find it.)

Picking the Right Seat

There are good seats and bad seats in poker, but it has nothing to do with how lucky the seat is. Rather, it has to do with where the seat is relative to different types of players.

Your ideal seat is one that gives you the best opportunity for winning the most money. Generally speaking, you want first crack at the biggest stack at the table. You also want to be positioned to see how the better and more aggressive players act before you act. A little observation of the players can help you pinpoint exactly which seat is likely to be most profitable for you.

Money usually moves around the table in a clockwise fashion, just as the dealing and betting action progresses. As the writer and poker theorist Mike Caro has pointed out, if you were to have a time-lapse camera film a cash poker game over the course of a few hours, you would see the stacks of chips shift around the table, growing and shrinking as the game progressed. The stacks would not grow uniformly. Some would only shrink. But if you watched a game for five to10 hours you would notice a loose and rough pattern. The stacks would appear to move like a wave around the table clockwise.

When a loose and wild player bets, the player to his immediate left has the first opportunity to win that money. Ideally, that player would be you. With the loose player to your right, you can re-raise his opening bet, which you know might not mean that he has good cards. It then makes it much more difficult for other players to enter the pot, and makes it much more likely that you will get to play the hand heads up against this weak player. And that's what you want: heads up action with the loose guy with the big stack. On the other hand, if that player happened to be to *your* immediate left, some other player might re-raise, making it much more difficult for you to manipulate the pot in a manner that increased your chances of winning. You'd almost surely have to fold all but your strongest hands, otherwise risk taking on two players. You can see that this would not be advantageous to you.

Simply put, you would like the most aggressive, loosest, and deepest stacks as close to your right as possible. You want first crack at these stacks!

By the same reasoning, you want to have passive, short-stacked, and extremely tight players to your left. They are unlikely to give you a difficult time once you have entered the pot. The passive players are unlikely to raise you, meaning that you can safely enter a hand without much fear that you will be raised by them. This is advantageous because you will generally know how much the round will cost you. Similarly, the short-stacked player won't present much risk to you as his maximum bet will only represent a small percentage of your stack. Finally, the extremely tight player is of little risk. Even if he is very aggressive or very tricky, he will seldom be in a hand. So even if his action is very hard to read, you will rarely be in a hand together, minimizing his impact on you in the game.

I realize that these instructions may at times create dilemmas for you. What if, for example, there are two seats available. The first has to its immediate right an extremely aggressive and loose player with a medium stack, while the other seat has a player with a huge stack to his right who appears very tight and not very good. Which of the two seats makes more sense? You'll regularly have to decide between options that are not clear-cut.

In general, when two seats are appealing for different reasons, I consider first the type of player I'm against, giving that precedence over stack size. I always want the excellent, loose-aggressive player on my right, even if he has a short stack. I presume that his stack size may change as his skill helps him accumulate chips from others.

Be willing to move your seat once you sit down. Most players are very sedentary. You should not feel the need to be. Once you sit down, continue to size up the players at the table. Think about where you would ideally like to sit based on the type of players you see and the chips they have. Recognize that you might change your mind, as players tend to come and go. Similarly, your assessment may change. The guy you thought was really good, and who tended to be in many hands with large bets and raises, may have suffered a few large losses and shut down. You might have wanted to move to his left but after watching what happened, it may no longer be in your best interests to do so. Just because you can move seats doesn't mean you should.

Exercise 6

Picking the Best Seat: aka "Left or Right?"
Here are some seating situations. This is a $2/5 game, with two empty seats, one on the left side of our object player, the other on his right. All the other players at the table are unknown and have roughly the same stack of chips, about $500.

1) The object player has a stack of more than $1,000 but you know nothing else about him. Do you sit on his left or right?

2) Same player, $500 stack. You've been watching him. He is tight and aggressive and seems good. He plays about one hand or two hands per orbit, usually from late position, and almost always enters for a raise or three-bet. Do you sit on his left or right?

3) Different player, $500 stack. He is extremely loose and aggressive, entering more than half of the pots. Left or right?

4) A fish with $2,000. Not very aggressive. Calls a lot. Seems relatively new to the game. Left or right?

5) A nit with $200 in perfectly stacked, largely untouched chips in front of him. Left or right?

6) A good but very tight player with $1,000. When he's in he's raising. Voluntarily enters pot less than one hand in 10. Do you sit to his left or right?

The following scenarios are more detailed. We have introduced some variety to the other players, but Seats 3 and 7 are available. You need to decide between the two. (If there is no further information, assume the players have a $500 stack and are moderately tight and moderately aggressive.)

7) The make-up of the table is as follows:

Seat 2: $500 stack (table average is about $400). Very passive and very loose.

Seat 4: $300 stack. Also passive and loose.

Seat 6: $1,000 stack. You've never seen him play a hand. You've watched 10 hands.

Seat 8: Best, most aggressive, least predictable player in the game. $500 stack. Plays a lot of hands. Tough to get a handle on.

Do you want Seat 3 or Seat 7?

8) The make-up of this game is as follows:

Seat 2: $300 stack. Very aggressive and active. You saw him get stacked twice. Just re-bought for $300.

Seat 4: $1,000 stack. About average in all respects.

Seat 6: $800 stack. Passive and moderately tight player.

Seat 8: $500 stack. Moderately aggressive, fairly tight. Seems to be a regular.

Do you want Seat 3 or Seat 7?

9) The make-up of this game is as follows:

Seat 2: $300 stack. Stereotypical retiree. Playing passively and tightly waiting for big cards.

Seat 4: $200 stack. Seems to be waiting to go home or lose his stack. Tight and passive.

Seat 6: $2,000 stack. You haven't seen him play a hand, but you know he must have, judging by his stack that is 4x average.

Seat 8: $1,000. Seems high or trying to prove that he is a maniac. Raises all the time, sometimes blind. Everyone is watching his action and he's lighting up the table.

Do you want Seat 3 or Seat 7?

Answers to Exercise 6

1) This one is easy. You want to sit after this player. When all things are equal, you want the seat to the left of the big stack.

2) Once again, you sit to his left. You generally want aggressive good players to act before you, so you can see what they do before you act. Though his stack is smaller than in the first example, it's still the size of yours, meaning that if you sit to his right, he might frequently be entering hands after you enter. He'll then have position on you and you will be at a disadvantage against this good player.

3) Once again, you want the seat on his left. A loose-aggressive player (a LAG) is an even more dangerous version of the prior player. If this player is on your left, you will frequently have to decide whether it's worth playing for what may be a raise after you, without much of a clue what his cards are. That's something you don't want to do if you don't have to. Sit to his left so you can size up his action before you act.

4) Once again, you want to sit to this player's left. You aren't afraid of his action, but rather eager to isolate him with your average and above average hands so you can then outplay him after the flop and take advantage of your position to exploit his generally weak play.

5) This is the perfect player to sit after you. He's hardly ever going to exert any pressure after you enter the pot. In those rare instances when he does enter, you will know he has a strong starting hand and can fold if he shows any post-flop enthusiasm for betting.

6) Right. Though you usually want good players on your right, the exception is if they are extremely tight. Since they hardly enter any hands, you really don't care how good they may be in the long run as you're rarely going to be in the same hands together.

7) Take the 3 seat. You have a tough opponent in Seat 8 and don't have a handle on him. You're just sitting down. Though Seat 6 is tempting with a $1,000 stack, you don't want to subject yourself to out-of-position contests all the time with the 8 seat. The 3 seat isn't ideal, but the $500 stack from a very loose and passive player is good, and the player after you in seat 4 is perfect.

8) You're best in the 7 seat. You've got two big-stacked players acting before you. They're not perfect opponents, but they're still better before you act than after you. The alternative seat leaves you with the big-stacked average player after you, and a very short stacked player acting before you. You're likely to have more profitable play in Seat 7.

9) Take Seat 3. No need to sit between the two big stacks when you first arrive. It's best to acclimatize first. You will see many hands where you'll have position on those two big stacks – every time the button is in the 3, 4, or 5 seat. Though you'll give up the opportunity to always play after the biggest stack, for all you know he may never be in any hands as he seems to be coasting after some earlier success.

While You're Waiting for a Game

You'll be eager to play when you arrive at the poker room. It's natural. Good for you. You are ready for competition.

But you may not get to sit down right away. There may be a waiting list, or the game you want may not have a seat. Either way, you might be cooling your heels with nothing to do. Don't worry. There are useful things you can do while you wait.

Read for Your Amusement or Edification

Bring a poker book and read. Perhaps you want to read about a game you don't play. Maybe there's a poker strategy book that you've heard is good. Maybe you want to go on a training site to review some hand examples that the commentator reviews. *What* it is doesn't matter as much as *that* it is. Why waste a minute? Come prepared to learn. I've also found it useful to bring my poker notebook, where I've logged notes about my session. This time waiting for a game is an excellent opportunity to review any lessons or insights I learned during my last session.

Go for a Walk

Poker players don't get enough exercise. Okay, maybe you're an exception. But with all of the sitting, either in poker rooms or at home while playing online, as a group we tend to be too sedentary. If your poker room doesn't have a pager/beeper system just plan on walking some pre-determined route that will have you walking in the vicinity, with many laps if necessary, so you'll always be close enough to come back to the brush every 5-10 minutes to check on where you are on the list. The walking doesn't have to be without learning either. You can read while you walk or, more safely, listen to a learning podcast or audio book to cram in some other learning.

Check out the Players in the Games

You don't know for sure where you'll be playing, but you can pick a table and start watching. You can make it worthwhile by testing your skills of observation:

♠ **Try to figure out a player.** Concentrate on watching them. Watch their action. How many times in an orbit do they fold pre-flop? How many times do they three-bet? If they had the initiative pre-flop, how many times did they continuation bet on the flop? Did they tend to call or fold to a raise or re-raise? In general, how tight were they? How passive were they? How much did they play in general? Try to keep track and then remember this for one player, then move on to another.

♠ **Count down the pot.** Try to figure it out as the betting goes forward. Try to remember it as you see the bets that are made. What's the typical raise? What is the typical bet after the flop? Figure it out in terms of percentage of the pot as well as in absolute terms. See if you can keep track of the size of the pot as it grows.

♠ **Put players on hand ranges.** Based on your observations, what do you think the ranges are of the players involved? Don't start with everyone. Try to pick one player at a time and watch him or her for a few hands. Then move on to other players. Ideally, you won't have more than 15 minutes or so to watch a table. Considering that, recognize that you're more likely to learn useful information by concentrating on a few players rather than diffusing your attention among many.

♠ **Think about where you'd ideally like to sit at the table.** Who is the most aggressive, trickiest player who is often in the hand? You'd probably want them on your right. Who are the tight timid players who exert little pressure or are in few hands? You'd probably want them on your left. Look at the stacks. Ideally you'd like the biggest ones on your right. In your mind, pick the ideal seat.

♠ **Watch the rake.** It's easy to get caught up in the hand when you're playing. But when you're watching, it's a perfect time to check and see when and how the rake is taken — and if it's taken correctly. See if you can spot the dealer taking money out of the pot, even as you're concentrating on the other players. Does the dealer ever take out too much? If he does, be ready to point it out when you sit down. Similarly, how is the dealer's pitch — the manner in which he actually physically deals the cards? Might he be inadvertently exposing cards to any of the players as he shuffles and deals? It's almost surely inadvertent, if it happens at all. Even so, be aware of it so you can either point it out when you are playing, or take advantage of it by sitting in an advantageous seat for seeing the exposed cards. (We'll deal with poker ethics elsewhere.)

Relax

Playing a solid poker game can be stressful and hard work. No one requires you to be working every minute of your time, including time waiting for a game. You are hereby given permission to use that time to relax and free up your brain so it will be at its peak when you do finally get in the game. I only suggest that if you relax, that you do so intentionally, and not just because you couldn't figure out what else to do, or as a habit.

You've waited patiently and productively, scoping out the best game, the best seat in that game, and the best players to exploit. You're ready to sit down. But how do you *play* a good game?

Chapter Two

Starting Hands – Keep it Tight

In this chapter we will look at a very rudimentary strategy for selecting which starting hands to play, and then how to play them. It will be based almost entirely on your position at the table, the presumed relative strength of your cards, and the betting action of your opponents. It is designed to be simple, straightforward, and easy to understand and implement. It will be useful in minimizing risk while you are developing your skills of observation and self-control.

What you'll learn: What cards to play, in what position, and how to play them.

Why it's important: Learning this tight-aggressive strategy will help rid you of bad habits and prepare you well for an even more effective method of play.

Introduction

Many experienced poker players have developed habits that are very hard to break. These habits often cost them money. We want to teach players - experienced veterans and those relatively new to the poker felt alike -

how to replace their habitual play with intentional and thoughtful play. Toward that end, I have stripped the game down to its essentials, and created a fairly simple and straightforward strategy for pre-flop play. It is very prescriptive.

Generally, you don't want absolute guidelines in poker. It is a very situation-specific game. The best answer, typically, to any poker question is, "It depends". Even so, it will be helpful at first to start you off with a very specific, narrow, and clear list of playable hands, with instructions of how to play them.

Admittedly, this is not optimal poker and your skills will eventually improve immeasurably from this starting point. But this strategy will be ideal while you are re-learning the game, and learning the skills of observation, discipline, and self control that you will eventually employ to your advantage.

This no limit hold'em strategy is meant to be simple and easy to implement. As you develop your powers of observation, and as you gain experience at the table, you will be able to add some flexibility to this system, broadening your pre-flop range for example, to better exploit particular habits of your opponents. But for now, we'll keep it very simple.

Table Position and Betting Actions

The language of poker is quite specific, with numerous terms having been created solely for use in the game. There are also some familiar words that have a particular use in poker, possibly different to how the words are used away from the tables. We'll take a quick look here at a few terms that will be repeated throughout the book, and which are especially relevant as we define our basic strategy.

The action you take in any hand will be determined initially by three things: your cards, your table position, and whatever your opponents have done before betting action reaches you. For the sake of clarity, I am repeating below the nomenclature I will use to refer to these things.

Table Position

Many seats around a poker table are assigned specific names. This aids with identification in hand analysis and discussion. In this text we're assuming a 10-person table with the following seating positions, starting to the immediate left of the dealer button:

Early Position		
Seat Number	**Seat Name**	**Abbreviation**
1	Small Blind	SB
2	Big Blind	BB
3	Under The Gun	UTG
4	Under The Gun+1	UTG+1

Middle Position		
Seat Number	**Seat Name**	**Abbreviation**
5	Under The Gun+2	UTG+2
6	Under The Gun+3	UTG+3
7	Lojack	LJ
8	Hijack	HJ

Late Position		
Seat Number	**Seat Name**	**Abbreviation**
9	Cutoff	CO
10	Button	BTN

When the description of play features only two players you may see "Hero" and "Villain". You are the Hero; your opponent is the Villain.

(Nomenclature for seating positions is not completely standardized. Some writers refer to the blinds as a group separate from early position. Some assign middle position to UTG+1, 2, and 3 – naming it MP1, MP2,

MP3. Some just use the seat numbers, and don't use names at all. The only slightly non-standard approach I have taken in this book is to group middle and late positions together for most strategy examples.)

Exercise 7

Here's a quick exercise to help you memorize these names for table positions. The black blob indicates the dealer seat.

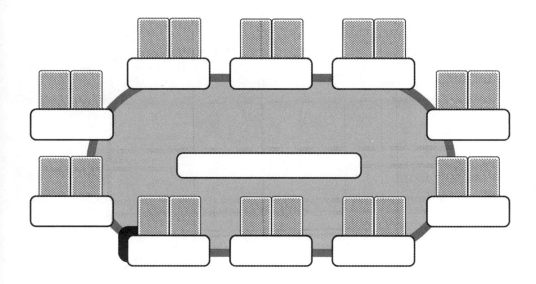

Find the button	Find the BB
Find UTG+3	Find the BTN
Find the big blind	Find the HJ
Find UTG	Find the small blind
Find the cutoff	Find the early position
Find the LJ	Find under the gun
Find the CO	Find late position
Find the SB	Find the blinds
Find the middle position seats	

Answers to Exercise 7

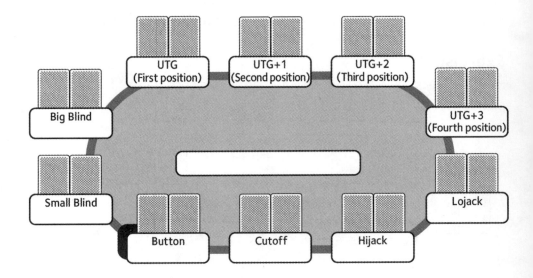

Betting Actions

In most betting rounds, one of three things might have happened before action reaches you:

- ♠ Folded to you (i.e., no one has volunteered any chips to the pot).
- ♠ Called by at least one player.
- ♠ Raised (or three-bet) by at least one player.

(A three-bet is a re-raise pre-flop. The BB is considered the first bet. The raise is considered the second bet. So the re-raise is generally referred to as a "three-bet". When that is then raised again, it's called a "four-bet", then a "five-bet", etc.)

Card Nomenclature

s = suited.
o = of different suits ("offsuit").

Example:

A-Ks = ace and king of same suits.

K-10o = king and 10 of different suits.

Cards are referred to by their number or first initial of their name. Ace is A, king is K, queen is Q, jack is J, ten is 10, then each number represents itself.

We are sometimes going to refer to more than one two-card hand at a time, using the following conventions.

♠ A-2+ means an ace and a two and every higher card. A-2, A-3 ... A-K.

♠ A-2s+ means an ace and every suited card. K-2s+ means a king and every suited card.

♠ 2-2+ means every pair 2-2 and higher.

♠ 4-4 to 8-8 would mean every pair, fours up to eights.

♠ J-J, K-K would mean a pair of jacks and a pair of kings exactly.

Which Hands to Play and From Where

We're now going to look at the kind of hands you should be playing – and the kind of hands you should be discarding – when you're sitting in each of the table positions. To repeat: when your skills improve, you can experiment with much more flexibility. But to start off, we're playing a very tight strategy.

Early Position Pre-Flop Play

Early position requires extremely strong starting cards, since you are likely to be in bad position against any opponent. Accordingly, you are going to play an extremely strong and narrow range.

Position: Early.
Action before: None.
Playable hands: A–K, Q–Q+.
What to do: Call with A–K, Raise with Q–Q+.

In an unraised pot, you are only going to play with these four hands: A–K (suited or unsuited), and a pair of queens or better. Q–Q+

In a typical game, if you open (i.e., you're the first person to volunteer chips to the pot) from early position, you're going to raise only with Q–Q+ – that's specifically Q–Q, K–K and A–A. You need to be aggressive to try to limit the field if you can, or, to build a pot that you expect to win.

You are not going to raise with A–K, because you do not yet have a hand that is expected to win. You will likely need to hit one of the six cards that improve A–K to what is usually the best hand on the flop. At this stage in your poker career, you are going to wait for the flop to see what develops before you commit many more chips to the pot.

Size of Your Raise

If you decide to raise, how much should you make it? You want to raise by an amount that is sufficient to get nearly all of your opponents to fold. Ideally, from early position, you'd like to be in last position and only play against one opponent over whom you have position: the SB, BB or sometimes UTG.

You may notice that there is a fairly standard amount of a pre-flop opening raise. It varies from player to player, and from game to game, but patterns develop. Typically, the amount of the raise is three or four times the size of the BB – so up to $10 or so in a typical $1/2 or $1/3 game. In some games it is more than this – sometimes considerably more. We're going to keep this simple. As a default, you will raise to $10 if there have been no calls before you act. If the player UTG has called, add one BB (big blind). So, for example, if you are UTG+1, and UTG has called the $2 BB, you should raise to $12.

If possible, you'd like to buy the button for this raise. By "buying the button" I mean that you'd like to knock out all of the players after you so that you'll be last to act for subsequent betting rounds.

Games vary in this regard for no discernable reason. I've played in games where the standard raise was to $7. Opponents respected the raise and folded as readily as if someone had made it $20. In other games it takes $20 to do the trick, maybe even $25 as the hour gets late and the drinking has an effect. So I'm suggesting you raise the amount – whatever it may be in the game you're in – that is most likely to get you last action. As a default, until you are confident that it should be some other amount, you will raise to $10.

Here's an example.

> You're in a $1/2 game and are UTG+1 with Q-Q.
> The player UTG calls the $2. The game is loose and you have a tight and aggressive image, as you play only about one hand in six or seven.

You'll make it $12 to go here, hoping that the players after you will fold and only the players who must act before you on later rounds – the small blind, big blind or UTG – will call. I realize that you might get a couple of loose players after you to call. But you want to make them pay for that privilege, since you estimate that your pair of queens is likely to be the best hand before the flop.

You're trying to avoid a lot of players calling your raise, and possibly improving on the flop to a hand that beats your queens. You'll be out of position for subsequent betting rounds, and will have to act before they do. This will put you at a disadvantage. For example, if an ace or a king flops, it may give them a higher pair than your queens. Even if it doesn't, the more players who see the flop, the higher the chance is that someone improves. If you "buy the button" and are the last to act, you will be able to see the reaction of your opponent or opponents before you decide what to do. This is a decided advantage.

You are going to call with A-K, suited or unsuited, with the hope that you'll hit a flush draw, two pair, a pair of aces, or a pair of kings with an ace kicker.

Exercise 8

Early Position Play 1

This is a very simple exercise. You are in early position in a $1/2 game and dealt the following hands. There has been no action ahead of you. Next to each hand indicate whether you should call, raise, or fold. If you believe the correct action is to raise, indicate the amount of your total bet.

1) J♥-10♠	11) 8♣-6♦	21) J♥-9♥	31) 3♥-3♣
2) K♦-Q♦	12) 7♠-2♠	22) Q♠-Q♦	32) J♦-9♦
3) A♥-3♥	13) J♥-J♦	23) 8♦-7♣	33) K♣-J♣
4) 7♠-7♣	14) K♠-K♥	24) A♣-4♠	34) A♠-A♦
5) A♠-Q♦	15) Q♥-10♥	25) A♣-J♠	35) A♠-K♠
6) A♠-K♦	16) A♣-9♣	26) A♣-Q♠	36) 6♥-6♦
7) 6♥-6♠	17) 8♠-8♦	27) A♣-K♠	37) 5♣-5♥
8) 9♣-8♣	18) 4♣-3♣	28) K♦-Q♦	38) Q♠-8♠
9) K♦-K♠	19) K♠-10♠	29) Q♠-J♠	39) Q♦-J♣
10) J♥-J♠	20) 9♦-9♣	30) 4♥-4♣	40) A♥-10♥

Answers to Exercise 8

Fold all but: 6-call, 9-raise, 14-raise, 22-raise, 27-call, 34-raise, 35-call. When you raise you will raise to $10.

Loose-passive Adjustment

Sometimes, if your game selection skills are very good, and if you are fortunate to have a lot of new or otherwise bad players in your game, there will be a lot of calling and very little pre-flop raising. I play in games like this all the time. When I go to a poker room, I always seek them out – and I usually find one.

When this is the case – when, typically, a majority of the players in your game only call the $2 or $3 big blind, then you can expand your pre-flop calling range in early position to include the pre-flop calling range from middle position. Specifically, when you adjust for a very loose-passive game, you will call with *all* pairs (2-2+), and all suited aces (A-2s+). You are hoping to flop a set with your pairs or the nut flush draw with your suited aces. (You may also flop two pair.)

Don't make a habit of this, and don't do it in games where it is common for players to raise pre-flop. When that is the case, or if the pot is raised before the action gets to you, you will fold cards in this broader range.

> **Position:** Early.
> **Action before:** One raise.
> **Playable hands:** A-A, K-K, Q-Q, A-K.
> **What to do:** Three-bet (re-raise) with A-A, K-K, Q-Q; Call with A-K.

You have already decided to play a very narrow range, anticipating that someone might raise after you. And you've already decided that you're playing your hand aggressively when you play. A raise before you act doesn't really change the landscape very much. You are still going to raise with those premium pairs, Q-Q+. And you're going to call with A-K (suited or unsuited).Similarly, let's keep our action extremely simple. With Q-Q, K-K, A-A, re-raise to three times their bet. With A-K call their raise and hope to connect with the flop.

If your raise is met with a three-bet or four-bet, just call with your entire range, except A-A. With A-A continue to raise and be prepared to get all your chips in.

Exercise 9

Early Position Play 2

In this exercise, you are UTG+1 in a $1/2 game, and are dealt the following cards. The scenario also describes the action prior to your decision. Unless otherwise stated, assume a typical game (not an especially loose and passive one) and assume all raises are to $10.

Assume all three-bets are to $30. Indicate what you do, and how much you raise (if appropriate).

1) J♥-J♠ folded to you.
2) K♥-J♥ one caller before you.
3) 9♠-9♦ one caller before you.
4) A♥-2♥ folded to you.
5) A♠-A♥ one raise before you.
6) A♥-K♦ folded to you.
7) Q♥-J♥ one raise before you.
8) Q♥-J♠ folded to you.
9) 2♠-2♥ one raise before you.
10) 8♠-8♥ one raise before you.
11) Q♥-Q♠ one caller before you.
12) Q♥-Q♦ a raise before you.
13) A♠-A♥ a raise before you, you three-bet, it is four-bet.
14) K♠-K♦ one call before you, you raise, you are three-bet.
15) Very loose passive game, 4♥-4♦, one call before you.
16) Very loose passive game, A♥-3♥, one raise before you.
17) Very loose passive game, 9-9, folded to you.
18) Very loose passive game, K-K, one call before you.
19) Very loose passive game, J-J, one call before you.
20) Very loose passive game, A-A, raised before you, you three-bet, it is four-bet.

Answers to Exercise 9
All folds except: 5 - raise to $30, 6 - call, 11 - raise to $12, 12 - call, 13 - five-bet, 14 - call, 15 - call, 17 - call, 18 - raise to $12, 19 - call, 20 - five-bet.

Middle Position Pre-flop Play
We'll move on now to your actions when you're sitting in middle position – i.e., UTG+2 through to the hijack seat. With more players to act before you pre-flop, there's a slightly longer list of things that might have happened before you need to make your first decision. However, your tight strategy doesn't change very much.

Position: Middle.
Action before: No raise.
Playable hands: All pocket pairs, A-2s+, A-Ko.
What to do: Raise with: J-J+; Call with: A-K, A-2s+, 2-2 to 10-10.

We'll keep this simple. You will play middle position as you play early position, with two adjustments. Firstly, if there's no raise before you, you'll broaden your raising range to include J-J. Secondly you'll broaden your calling range to include all pocket pairs up to 10-10, as well as A-2s+. Other than that, the main difference between middle-position and early-position play will be due to the frequency of the calls and possibility of raises before it is your turn to act. So your raise, taking those likely additional callers into account, will frequently be larger than the raises in early position. For example, if you are in the LJ (lojack) with Q-Q, and three players call the $2 big blind, you will raise not to $10, but to $16.

Position: Middle.
Action before: Raised.
Playable hands: Q-Q+, A-K and, possibly, A-2s+, 2-2 to J-J.
What to do: Raise with Q-Q+; Call with A-K; Also call with A-K, A-2s+, 2-2 – J-J if you meet the criteria explained below.

There is a stronger possibility in middle position, when compared with early position, that the pot will be raised before action gets to you. When you have Q-Q+ you will raise to three times the bet. When you have A-K you will call.

With inferior hands, you will call if the situation meets the following criteria:

♠ The preceding raise is no more than 7 BBs.

♠ The effective stack is at least 15 times the bet.

(A quick note about effective stacks: An "effective stack" is the size of your stack or the size of your opponent's stack, whichever is smaller. It's called "effective stack" because when you bet, the only amount you may effectively bet is the amount that your opponent may call. If you have $1,000 but your opponent only has $100, you are effectively limited to betting $100 – since he may call no more than the $100 he has in front of him. Your additional $900 in your stack is effectively irrelevant.)

You are not going to call a raise of more than 7BB because you believe that the raiser is trying to protect his strong hand with that uncharacteristically large raise. As mentioned earlier, it may be that the "standard" raise for your game has just migrated to this large number – and that it doesn't represent anything. It may be that the raiser is just being particularly wild. No matter. You're going to play it safe at this level. You will not call with any of your more speculative hands for this amount.

There are times when you will call, however. Hitting either a set or a flush draw happens around 11 percent of the time and you have a chance to win a very large pot when it does. It's likely to be a pot large enough to more than compensate you for the many times you'll call and fold to a bet on the flop.

But it's important to make sure that you make this call only if the effective stack in the hand is 15 times the bet or more. You need to make sure the potential pot you could win is big enough. For example, if someone raises to $10, you will need an effective stack of at least $150 to take full advantage of the few times you will hit your hand on the flop. We'll cover this more under "implied odds", but recognize that it's not enough to just have the potential of winning more money on future streets. You actually have to develop a technique for extracting that extra money from your opponent when you improve.

Exercise 10

Middle Position Play
You are in middle position and receive the hands listed below. Indicate your betting action for each hand, assuming you have an effective stack of $200.

1) J♥-J♠ folded to you.
2) K♥-J♥ one caller before you.
3) 9♠-9♦ one caller before you.
4) A♥-2♥ folded to you.
5) A♠-A♥ raise of 5BB before you.
6) A♥-K♦ folded to you.
7) Q♥-J♥ raise of 3BB before you.
8) Q♥-J♠ folded to you.
9) 2♠-2♥ raise of 8BB before you.
10) 2♠-2♥ raise of 3BB before you.
11) Q♥-Q♠ one call before you.
12) Q♥-Q♦ raise of 5BB before you.
13) A♠-A♥ raise of 3BB before you, you three-bet 9BB, it is four-bet 20BB and action is to you.
14) K♠-K♦ one call before you, you raise 5BB, you are three-bet to 12BB.
15) 7♥-7♦ three calls before you.
16) 10♦-10s two calls before you.
17) K♠-K♥ three calls before you.
18) J♥-J♦ two calls before you.
19) Q♠-Q♥ one call and a raise to $10 before you.
20) A♠-K♥ two calls and a raise to $12 before you.

Answers to Exercise 10

1) Raise to $10.	8) Fold.	15) Call.
2) Fold.	9) Fold.	16) Call.
3) Call.	10) Call.	17) Raise to $16.
4) Call.	11) Raise to $12.	18) Raise to $14.
5) Raise to 15BB.	12) Raise to 15BB.	19) Three-bet to $30.
6) Call.	13) Move all-in.	20) Call.
7) Fold.	14) Call.	

Positon: Middle and Late.
Action before: Raised and three-bet.
Playable hands: Q-Q+.
What to do: Raise three times three-bet with A-A, K-K; Call with Q-Q.

Some other things might have happened if you're in middle or late position. Sometimes you will face a raise and a three-bet before action gets to you. You need to play only your strongest range when that is the case.

When there is a three-bet, and the action is to you, fold every hand except A-A, K-K and Q-Q. Raise three times their bet with A-A and K-K. Call with Q-Q. Fold everything else, including A-K.

Don't get cute and slow-play your aces or kings. Raise with them. You'll find that many players with lesser hands will call anyway, which is what you want. But if all of your opponents fold to your three-bet, that's okay too.

What you don't want to do is call the three-bet, trying to trap other players into the hand. There is just too much improvement that is possible on the flop for you to do this. True, when you get better and can better put your opponent on a range of hands, and outplay him on the flop, maybe then you can mix up your play. But for now, just be very aggressive with those kings and aces!

In the event that you are four-bet, fold everything but aces – and move all-in with them!

Exercise 11

Middle and Late Position Play
The pot has been raised to $10 and three-bet to $30 before action reaches you in the lojack seat. . You have an effective stack of $200. What is your action?

1) K♥-J♥
2) 10♠-9♠
3) A♣-Q♠
4) A♣-Q♣
5) A♥-J♥

6) A♠-A♣
7) K♥-K♦
8) J♥-J♠
9) 8♦-8♥
10) 4♣-4♦

11) J♣-10♣
12) Q♥-Q♣
13) 9♦-9♣
14) A♥-K♥
15) A♠-K♦

Answers to Exercise 11
Fold all of your hands except: 6 – raise to $90; 7 – raise to $90; 12 – call.

Exercise 12
Imagine the same scenario as above, except the raises were as follows: Raise to $6; raise to $12.

1) K♠-J♠
2) 10♣-9♣
3) A♦-Q♥
4) A♠-J♠
5) A♥-A♦

6) K♣-K♦
7) J♥-J♠
8) 8♠-8♣
9) 4♣-4♦
10) J♠-10♣

11) J♠-10s
12) Q♥-Q♦
13) 9♣-9♥
14) A♥-K♥
15) A♠-K♦

Answers to Exercise 12
The amount of the raise and three-bet is immaterial at this point. You are going to respond in the same way – folding everything but your three premium pairs – Q-Q+. You will four-bet with your kings and aces and call with your queens.

Late Position Pre-flop Play

> **Position:** Late.
> **Action before:** Variable.
> **Playable hands:** All pocket pairs; A-2s+, suited connectors 7-6s+; two Broadway cards; two-gapped flush cards 6-8s+.
> **What to do:** Raise with 8-8+, A-2s+, two Broadway cards; Call with 2-2 – 7-7, suited connectors 7-6s+, two-gapped flush cards 8-6s+.

We are looking at just two spots for our late position: the cutoff seat (CO) and the button (BTN). From these positions, in a typical game, we're playing a much broader range of hands than in early and middle position, and we're playing them more aggressively.

Late position is ideal, especially if the betting action moves to you without any opponent raising. This should give you greater confidence to play a selection of hands that you would instantly fold from early or middle position.

In an un-raised pot – i.e., a pot in which everyone preceding you has either folded or only called – raise with the following range: 8-8+, A-2s+, and any two Broadway cards. We will stick to the policy of raising 3BB plus 1BB for every caller.

In an unraised pot, call with the following range: 2-2 to 7-7, suited connectors that are not raising hands, one and two-gapped flush cards 8-6s+. Fold everything else.

If you call and are raised, or if you are raised and then three-bet, you will raise again with A-A and K-K, call with all other pairs and your suited aces, and call with A-K. (You will call if the circumstances are as described in the prior section for middle and late position.) You will fold everything else.

Admittedly, these rules are all somewhat arbitrary and they are also extremely tight. Even so, before you are able to get a read on your opponents, or understand how their image of you affects their play, you will play it very, very safe. As you develop as a player you will eventually take many factors into consideration including your read of the raiser and your read of their read of you. Still, my experience is that in games with beginning, inexperienced, poor or otherwise typical low-limit players, these ranges work best. I'd rather you concede your other hands before the flop for a large bet than run the risk that you are dominated during the next betting rounds. Again, there will be exceptions that you'll be able to exploit eventually. But for now, my advice is to take the safer route when confronted with players who play back at you after you've been aggressive.

One Exception for the CO Position

When you are the cutoff, you are willing to raise with your marginal hands (those other than premium pairs and A-K) because you think your raise is likely to knock out the button – buying you last position on all subsequent betting rounds. Sometimes this is not the case. Sometimes, the player on your immediate left is either very aggressive, very good, or otherwise not likely to fold when you raise. When that is the case, play from the cutoff as though it is a middle position seat.

Playing Against Raises (All Positions)

The question may arise as to what to do if you call with one of these A-2s+ or 2-2+ hands (or an even a weaker hand in late position) and someone after you raises.

The simple answer is that in most circumstances, in a typical game, at this stage of your poker education, you will tend to fold. You may be out of position; the raiser will tend to have a legitimate hand that may dominate your hand; and his raise will tend to thin the field – perhaps to just the two of you. You don't want that. That's one of the reasons you didn't raise yourself.

Even so, there are circumstances when you will call the raise – specifically when *three* of the following five criteria are fulfilled:

- ♠ The raise is by less than 8BB.
- ♠ You believe at least one other player will call.
- ♠ Your effective stack is at least 15 times the total bet.
- ♠ You don't think the raiser is an excellent player.
- ♠ You will have position on the raiser.

Here are some examples of how you'd make a calculation based on the above criteria.

> Two players call the $2 BB. You have 4♦-4♥ in the CO.
> You call the $2 BB. The BTN, an average player, raises to
> $15. Everyone folds to you. You have an effective stack
> of $200.

Apply the five tests above:

- ♠ The raise is to 7.5BB. That's okay.

- ♠ The pot will be heads up. That's one strike

- ♠ Your effective stack of $200 is only 13.33 times the total bet.
  That's two strikes.

- ♠ The button is an average player. That's okay, but alone, it's not
  enough to call.

- ♠ You will not have position on the raiser. Strike three. Fold!

Here's another scenario.

> Two players call the $2 BB. You have 4♦-4♥ in the CO
> and call the $2 BB. The BTN raises to $10. Both players
> who called the BB call the additional $8. You have an
> effective stack of $200.

Apply the five tests above:

- ♠ The raise is to 5BB. You can call it.

- ♠ There are two players who have already called it. That's good. The
  pot will be at least four-way. You can call it.

- ♠ Your effective stack of $200 is 20 times the $10 bet. You can call
  it.

♠ The button is an average player. You can call it.

♠ The button will have position on you. Not good, but four other criteria are met.

You only needed three criteria and you've got four. You should call. Here's another scenario.

> You're UTG+2 with A♦-K♣. The two players before you fold, you call and three other players call, including the SB. The BB, a very aggressive and seemingly excellent player, raises to $15. Action is to you.

Apply the five tests:

♠ The raise is only 7.5 BB. You could call if you could find two other factors that would allow you to call.

♠ You're not sure if the other players will call.

♠ Your effective stack is not large enough. This counts against you calling.

♠ You think the raiser is an excellent player. This counts against you calling.

♠ You will have position on the raiser. This counts in your favor.

You have two factors in your favor – position on the raiser and a bet that is less than 8BB. On the other hand he is an excellent player, you don't have a large enough multiple of his bet, and you don't know if the hand will be played multi-way. Folding is the best option.

In general, you want to make sure that there is a lot of money to be won if you hit your relatively long-shot draw to a set or a flush draw. You don't want to have to invest too much money to see that draw. And you don't want to be out of position against someone whom you think can probably outplay you on the flop, turn, and river.

One more word about this. You will sometimes hear that you can call a pre-flop raise with a pair if your effective stack is at least eight times the raiser's bet. The theory is that since, on average, you will only hit a set 12% of the time or so, that when you do hit a set you can win your opponent's stack – so the bet will be worth it if you have eight times his stack to win. That's the theory. But things don't really work that way in reality. In reality, you may hit your set, you may bet, and your opponent may fold and you win nothing more. Or you may make a single bet on the turn that he'll call, but he'll fold on the river. There may be any of a number of scenarios where you are unable to extract his full stack. The fact that you *might* win his stack is no assurance that you *will* win his stack when you hit your set. Hence, from my experience, until you are an experienced and competent veteran, with the special skill of getting maximum value for your sets, I want the other criteria in place.

Accordingly, to play it safe, you really need to make sure the other criteria are being met. You want a much larger stack to win (15 times the bet). You'd like a third player in the hand. You want position. You want an opponent who is not already identified as a great player. And you want a bet that by itself does not seem to represent an extremely strong hand.

Bottom line: When there's a raise play very cautiously. But when it looks like there's a chance to make a lot of money for relatively little risk, go ahead and see the flop.

Chapter Three

Playing the Flop

In this chapter we will build upon the rudimentary strategy we learned for pre-flop play, and develop a strategy for when the first three community cards are out. While not as prescriptive as the pre-flop strategy, we will still focus on straightforward strategy, without much deception – though play does become more complicated.

What you'll learn: How to best exploit your opponents as the hand progresses, using a straightforward and relatively simple strategy.

Why it's important: You need to understand how best to follow through on your tight-aggressive pre-flop strategy, with effective post-flop play.

Introduction

We kept your pre-flop range very narrow, and your play tight and aggressive. In part, this was to ensure that your post-flop decisions are relatively simple. Even so, play on the flop will not be as prescriptive as the pre-flop strategy we've already laid out. You will need to understand drawing odds and pot odds, and you'll need to fully understand what a continuation bet is and when it should be employed.

Play on the Flop

You will have reached the flop in one of the following situations:

♠ As the pre-flop aggressor.

♠ After calling the pre-flop aggressor with a drawing hand.

First, let's define our terms.

The *pre-flop aggressor* is the person who last escalated action before the flop. So, for example, if you had Q♥-Q♦ in the HJ seat and raised an un-raised pot and were called by three people, you would be the pre-flop aggressor.

A *drawing hand* is a hand that needs to improve to win. So, for example, A♥-3♥ pre-flop is a drawing hand.

You also need to understand drawing odds and pot odds. We'll deal with these in more detail in Chapter 4, but a brief summary should suffice for now.

Drawing odds are the odds against you making your hand. For example, if you have A♥-3♥ and the flop is K♥-7♥-6♣, the odds against you making your flush on the next card are roughly 4-to-1. (See the drawing odds chart on page 96.) But you need to understand that those are the odds *against* you making your hand. Another way to think of it is that in five tries, you are likely to make your flush once. One out of five tries is the same as 4-to-1.

Pot odds is the ratio of the size of the pot to the size of the bet you must call to see your next card. For example, if there is $40 in the pot from pre-flop betting and your opponent bets $20, you are getting 3-to-1 pot odds for your call. The pot will be $60 ($40 plus his $20 bet) and you will need to call $20. That's a $60 pot compared with your $20 bet. 60-to-20. Simplified, that's 3-to-1.

We'll deal with how to play your drawing hands first.

Playing Drawing Hands on the Flop

If you have a drawing hand pre-flop, it is far more likely that you miss your draw than hit it. That's the first, important lesson you need to know about post-flop play. And here's what to do when that happens.

When You Miss Your Hand and your Opponent Bets

When you called an aggressor with a drawing hand pre-flop, and did not hit your hand, and your opponent bets, you should generally fold. You will not try to outplay your opponent with cleverness or deception. You will not worry about his range and how your hand does against it. You will assume that their bet pre-flop and post-flop bets meant strength, you will recognize that your hand has not improved, and you will therefore fold to avoid any further losses.

Accordingly, you will fold to any aggression on the flop unless you have a very strong draw (generally to the nut straight or flush) – and then only if you have the pot odds to do so.

Here are some examples of drawing hands that you should be prepared to give up.

> The player in the HJ called pre-flop. You also called in the CO with A♥-5♥. The BB raised to $12. HJ called and you called. The flop was K♠-9♦-5♠. BB bets $20. HJ folds.

You should fold.

Yes, you have bottom pair and an over-card. Yes, your opponent may not have hit anything and may have raised pre-flop with nothing. You really don't know. Don't worry about it. You didn't hit your hand as you had intended. (You hoped for two pair or a flush draw.) Don't over-think this. Fold to the bet.

> The player UTG called and you called in the HJ with
> 7♠-7♣. CO called before BTN raised to $10. BB called,
> UTG called. You called. CO called. The flop was
> A♦-8♠-6♠. It's checked to you. All players, including
> you, check to the BTN. He bets $25. UTG calls. Action is
> to you. What do you do?

You should fold. Yes, you have three cards to a straight flush, and it looks good. Yes, you have a pair that is higher than bottom pair. Yes, there's $100 in the pot, so you're getting 4-to-1 on your call. No matter. You were drawing for a set – also known as "set-mining" – and you missed. To make matters worse, the pre-flop aggressor bet again. You should fold.

It is very easy to think of examples of when you miss your hand. You had a medium or small pair and were drawing for a set and missed your set. Your opponent bets. Fold. You had two to a flush and you didn't hit a flush draw. Fold, even if you hit bottom pair and even if you hit a back-door flush draw (i.e., you had three to a flush).

You are not going to get clever. You are going to wait for a better opportunity.

When You Miss and your Opponent Checks

You should still resist the urge to get tricky if you miss your hand, even if your opponent checks. You may be tempted to steal the pot by betting into his apparent weakness. But don't. You should not bluff just because you can. You will generally check behind and see another card for free. There are exceptions. I'll cover them below under "deception". But for now, if you don't hit a strong hand or a strong draw on the flop, your default is to check if it is checked to you and fold if it is bet to you.

When You Hit your Draw: Sets

If you are fortunate enough to have called with a pair pre-flop, drawing to a set, and have now hit one of the two cards that could improve your hand, you want to make as much money as possible. There are rare instances when you will be against another set or even a stronger hand, but it is usually fair to assume you have the best of it. The vast majority of the time you will be far ahead of your opponents.

In general, your action will be:

- ♠ Call if there is a bet in front of you

- ♠ Check to the pre-flop bettor if you are first to act

- ♠ Bet about a third of the pot if the action is checked to you.

You want to bet in late position if it's checked to you, even though it may result in everyone folding. Yes, that might feel as though you haven't extracted maximum value for your great hand. But that's okay. You will have won the pot. There's also a good possibility that your opponents will suspect that you're trying to steal the pot from late position, causing them to call you – and perhaps even raise you. This will make it more likely that they will also call on the turn and river, as the pot will become an increasingly larger target.

When You Hit Your Draw: Nut Flushes and Nut Flush Draws

Once in a while – a little less than one percent of the time – you will draw with two suited cards and flop a flush. You will play this exactly as you played a set: you check unless you are last to act and it has been checked to you, in which case you will bet a third of the pot. Again, you will give your opponents a chance to bet first. But if the betting round looks like it will pass without a bet, you should bet from late position. It is likely to be viewed as a steal attempt.

Much more frequently, though still not commonly (about 11 percent of the time, to be precise) you will draw with your A-2s+ and hit two of your suit. This is also good, though not as good as hitting a set. Nine cards remain in the deck that will give you the flush, and you'll hit one more than a third of the time.

In general, though this is still very much a drawing hand, you will play it the same way as you would play your set. You will:

♠ Call if there is a bet in front of you

♠ Check to the pre-flop bettor if he has position on you

♠ Bet about a third of the pot if the action is checked to you.

However, unlike when you hit a set, you will not call if there is a bet and a raise in front of you. You still only have a drawing hand, after all. Similarly, you will not call any bet unless you are fairly sure that you will be able to make at least twice the price of the call. Here are some examples of when you should fold.

> Your opponent raises to $10 in early position pre-flop. You have an effective stack of $300. Two players call the raise as do you, with A♥-10♥. The flop is K♥-8♥-2♠. The pre-flop raiser bets $25. The first opponent calls the $25 and the next player raises to $100. Don't call this raise. You don't know what the action will be after you. You're not assured of getting 2-to-1 if you hit your hand.

You should fold (even though it's tempting to call).

> You are in for $15 pre-flop with A♥-2♥ in the CO. (You followed a few callers, the BTN raised and two of you called.) You have a stack after the calls of $100. The flop is Q♥-9♥-7♠ and is checked to you. You check as the pre-flop raiser has position on you. The BTN, with $300 in his stack, bets your stack of $100.

Don't call. Fold. You are not going to get 2-to-1 on your money if you hit. You can't. You'd be all-in for $100 with a pot of $145. You might ask why the villain was betting so much. He might be bluffing. But you're not going to find out. You're going to fold because you don't yet have a hand and you only have a 36 percent chance of hitting your hand by the river. It's not worth it. Fold.

On the other hand, here are situations when you should *call*.

> You are on the button pre-flop with A♦-7♦. Everyone folds to the LJ who raises to $10. Two players call as do you. The flop is J♠-10♦-3♦. LJ bets $20. HJ folds. CO calls the $20.

Go ahead and call. You are already getting 4-to-1 on your money. (The pot is $83 at this point. Your call of $20 gives you a little better than 4-to-1 odds). And if you hit your flush you may make quite a bit more.

> Same hand. The LJ bets $30. HJ folds. CO calls the $30. You can still call. The pot is $100. Your call is $30.

It's a good bet considering you're drawing with a 36 percent chance to win (better than 2-to-1) by the river. Even if your opponent bets the pot of $40, and all other opponents fold, you can still call. You're getting 2-to-1 exactly on your call ($80 for your $40 call), and you have a better chance than that of hitting your flush by the river (36 percent to 64 percent). Plus, there's the extra money you can make if you do hit your flush.

Making Other Hands with the Nut Flush Draw
In addition to the times you hit a flush or a flush draw, there are a three other hands worth playing on the flop.

Hitting Aces Up (Without Board Pairing)
Occasionally you will pair your ace and your kicker, in which case you should bet a little more than half the pot from any position. This is a made

hand and you want to bet it for value. If you are re-raised be inclined to call unless you think you might be against a bigger two pair. This will sometimes be the case if there is another Broadway card on the flop to go with the ace, and you have a lower second pair.

> For example, imagine you have A♥-7♥ in the LJ, you called the $2 BB pre-flop, were raised to $12 by the button, the BB called the $12 and you called. You now see a flop of A♠-K♦-7♣. You hit aces up – aces over 7♠ to be precise. The BB checks. You bet $25 and get raised to $60 by the BTN (whom you judge to be at least a fairly good player). The BB folds and it's your action.

Unless the BTN is a dunderhead, it's likely that he has you dominated with the top two pair, A-K. True, he might have A-Q – and with top pair top kicker he figures you have a lower kicker like A-J or A-10. True, he might be raising as a bluff (or if the board brought a potential flush draw, a semi-bluff). True, he might be hoping to push you and the other players around with very aggressive play. But unless you know your opponent well, and he is at least somewhat tricky, that's probably not the case. His raising range pre-flop probably included A-K. His raising range now almost surely does.

If you're in the American West and you hear a galloping herd, but can't see anything, think horses, not zebras.

On the other hand, if the flop doesn't include a Broadway card, and you bet your two-pair and get raised, it's more likely that the raiser has top pair and top kicker – and you are ahead. In the hand above, for example, if the flop were A♠-7♣-2♦, then you'd have top two pair, and your opponent's raising range would most likely be A-J, A-Q, and A-K, thinking he had you out-kicked.

If the board pairs, your aces up is only worthwhile if it is top two pair or two pair with the top kicker. So for example, if you have A♦-J♦ and the flop were A♠-7♣-7♦, you have two pair but it loses to anyone with A-K,

A-Q, (or, of course, A-7 or any other hand with a seven). If there is action to you, or after you bet, give them credit for a better hand and fold. On the other hand, if you have A-K with the same flop, you will only be behind someone with A-7 (or the very rare instance of someone holding a seven or two aces). You should bet, and if you are raised – even if substantially so – you should call.

Hitting a Pair of Aces without Top Kicker
If you flop a pair of aces but have kicker trouble, you still want to bet this hand if you are first to act, but you should be prepared to play it more cautiously. Your bet sizing should be a little more than half the pot, but if you are raised, you should tend to fold this hand unless you have good reason to believe that your opponent is extremely reckless and poor. If the pre-flop aggressor bets, fold. Yes, it's true that he may just be continuing to bet with a lower pair, with two big cards that did not pair, or with a middle or lower pair. Even so you are better off, for now, before you have mastered your reads, to assume he raised pre-flop with a bigger ace and now has you dominated with two pair or a higher kicker. Wait until you are confident that you have the better hand.

When You Were the Pre-Flop Aggressor and You are First to Act Post-Flop
When you see a flop as the pre-flop aggressor, you generally then find yourself in one of four situations:

- ♠ Your strong pre-flop hand does not improve, but you believe it is still good
- ♠ Your strong pre-flop hand improves to an extremely strong hand
- ♠ Your pre-flop drawing hand improves to a strong hand
- ♠ Your pre-flop drawing hand does not improve to a strong hand

Let's look at each of these in turn.

1) Your Strong Pre-flop Hand Did Not Improve but is Probably Still Good

This is a situation when you raised or three-bet with a premium pair, did not improve on the flop, but now have to make your post-flop decision either in first position or after your opponent(s) has checked to you.

You should bet a little more than half the pot. Here's a simple example.

> A few players called the BB, you raised the BB on the BTN with J-J and the HJ called you. The flop is A♠-10♦-9♣. The HJ checks.

You believe your hand is still good because your opponent checked. True, he may have checked with a weak ace. But when you look at the full range of possibilities, that is only one of many. He may have started with so many hands pre-flop – a huge range – that we have to assume his check means his range is still very broad and weak. With such a broad and weak range, you must bet. You can't risk giving him a free turn card. Your sizing should be a little more than half the pot. Here's another example.

> You raised UTG+2 with Q-Q and the BTN called. Everyone else folded. The flop is A♠-10♦-9♣. You are first to act.

You should bet a little more than half the pot.

The rationale is simple. With only three aces out there, and all but one opponent having folded, you think you are still in the lead. You don't want your opponent to draw cheaply against you and hit his hand. So whether or not your opponent has yet acted, make a substantial bet. If he calls he will tend to have the worst of it. If he folds and you win the pot, good for you.

If you are raised, you should probably fold. The raise helps narrow the likely range of your opponent. It becomes likely that he called your pre-flop raise with an ace and has now hit one. He may have A-K, A-Q, A-J, etc. This is another reason to make a substantial bet pre-flop – at least a little more than half the size of the pot. If you make a smaller bet, your opponents may be tempted to play back at you with less than an ace because it's relatively cheap to do so. Keep the post-flop bet stiff to diminish the chances they'll play games with a cheap raise.

2) Your Strong Pre-flop Hand Improved on the Flop to an Extremely Strong Hand

Imagine, for example, you raised pre-flop with pocket queens and there was a third queen on the flop. As a general practice, you should continue to bet. At this level, with a generally loose and passive table, and with the bad players you should be looking to play against, your bet on the flop will tend to be called enough times to warrant the risk that everyone might fold to your bet. So make the bet unless at least *one* of the following criteria are met.

- ♠ You have top set: With top set, slow play and check, and hope that someone else leads the betting, in which case call. With top set you are willing to allow opponents to improve on the next card. So, in the example of your Q-Q pre-flop becoming a set of queens, tend to bet it with a flop of A♥-Q♥-8♠ or K♥-Q♠-8♦. Check it if the flop is Q♠-8♣-2♦.

- ♠ You hit a set and it's a dry board: With a set and no straight or flush draws on the board, it's okay to slow-play your set. With 10-10 and a flop of A♠-10♥-6♦ you could check.

- ♠ There's already action: with a set and action to you, it's okay to just call. You will save your aggression for the turn.

- ♠ You are heads up against a tight or timid player: with a set against one opponent you are likely to be far enough ahead to warrant a check. This is true even with a wet board. If a straight or a flush hit you will still have 10 outs to pull ahead of your lone opponent.

3) Your Pre-flop Drawing Hand Improves to a Strong Hand

This would typically occur when you were in late position and raised pre-flop with a strong drawing hand when the pot was not raised in front of you. The flop hit and your opponents checked to you, in last position (typically, you will have knocked out the one opponent remaining in the button).

You will bet, a little more than half the pot as you would in the other betting examples. You are representing the best hand. If your opponents call, they are paying a significant price to see the turn. If they fold you win.

The exception to the above is if you bet your drawing hand and hit an extremely strong hand. If, for example, you played your suited ace and hit the nut flush on the flop, or if you played a suited connector and hit a full-house, or you played a low pair and hit quads. In those instances, of hitting extremely unusual and strong hands, you will check the flop.

4) Your Pre-flop Drawing Hand does not Improve to a Strong Hand

You will only be in this situation when you are in late position – on the button or in the cutoff. In all other positions you would call with your strong drawing hands.

Most of the time, you will have last action, as your pre-flop raise will have succeeded in buying you the button. When that is the case, you will be in a situation of deciding whether or not to continue with your aggression on the flop, even though you have not hit your hand. Before you can decide that, you must understand two critical concepts – board texture and continuation bets. I describe them below.

Continuation Bets (C-bets)

Continuation bets, often known simply as c-bets, are bets made after the flop by the person who was the last aggressor pre-flop. Typically that will be the initial raiser, but possibly also the player making a three-bet or four-bet.

A c-bet supposedly indicates that a player considers his hand is still best, but this might not always be the case. On many occasions, a c-bet is an act of deception. It will often be a form of a bluff. A player might c-bet whether or not he has hit the flop.

A c-bet is usually a little more than half the pot – enough to convince your opponents that you have something, but no so much that you can't get away from the hand if the c-bet doesn't work.

It should generally be about the same size whether it's a bluff or a value bet – so your opponent can't tell the difference between the two. So if you bet half to two-thirds the size of the pot when you hit your hand, you should bet the same when you do not.

There are Advantages and Disadvantages to Making C-bets

Most of the time, the opponents who called you pre-flop will not hit the flop. The chief advantage to making a c-bet is that you will win the pot when your opponents, unimproved, fold to your bet. Thus, a bet after the flop will tend to get unsophisticated, straightforward players who aren't thinking about how you are likely to play your hand, to fold their unimproved hand – awarding you the pot in the process. This allows the player making the c-bet to win a pot that has been enriched by pre-flop calls – even when he hasn't been hit by the flop. That's a very big advantage!

Here's an example of that strategy in action.

> You are in the cutoff with A♥-10♥. Four players call the BB. You raise to $18. UTG+2 calls your raise and there's $42 in the pot. The flop is K♥-8♠-4♣. UTG+2 checks to you. Though you have nothing more than an over-card to the board and a backdoor flush draw, you c-bet $25. Your opponent probably missed the flop and will fold.

Yes, it's true that your opponent might have been helped by this flop. He could be checking with the intention of calling your bet – or even raising you. But much more likely, he had some drawing hand pre-flop that failed to sufficiently improve on the flop. Your $25 bet will generally convince him to fold.

Disadvantages and Risks of Making a C-bet

If you c-bet too frequently, many of your opponents (even relatively bad opponents) will start to notice it – and suspect your bet on the flop doesn't mean you have improved. They then may take countermeasures – like calling your c-bet and then betting or raising the turn, or raising your c-bet on the flop, knowing you often have nothing.

Another risk is that you may not have the self-control to get away from your hand when your opponent uncharacteristically shows strength after you c-bet. Here's an example.

> You started with A♠-6♠ on the button. The players UTG+2 and in the LJ seat called the BB. The other players folded. When the action reached you on the BTN you raised to 5BB. The BB, UTG+2, and LJ called. The flop is K♠-9♦-6♣. All three opponents check. As is your habit, you confidently make a c-bet of 15BB. The BB folds. Your UTG+2 opponent raises you to 40BB – a check-raise. LJ folds.

You may be tempted to call him. Don't. Unless you have an extremely loose and aggressive image or he is a completely unpredictable maniac you should fold.

It's tempting to call – and many players, once they have made their c-bets, feel obliged to at least see the turn. There's no obligation. Fold to a check-raise like this.

Similarly, you might have been banking on taking the pot away with a c-bet, only to have your opponent preempt you on the flop. Imagine the above situation before the flop. But on the flop, K♠-9♦-6♣, after the BB checks UTG+2 bets 20BB right out of the chute. LJ folds. What do you do?

Sure, with your A♠-6♠ you paired your six and you have an ace over-card to the board and a backdoor nut flush draw. But think about UTG+2's likely range. Start by remembering how he played pre-flop. He called your pre-flop raise, out of position, after the BB called. So he started with something at least fairly strong – a pair, a couple of big cards, a suited ace maybe. Then think about how he's acting on the flop. After the flop your opponent is still facing three opponents – only one of whom has shown indifference to the flop by checking. With two players yet to act, and out of position, his 20BB bet shows it's highly unlikely that he's bluffing – considering the other opponents and his early position. You've got to think he's considerably stronger than a pair of sixes to bet into you (a donk bet as it's sometimes called), after you were the pre-flop aggressor. His range surely consists of a big pair (10-10 to Q-Q), K-2+, (which would give him a pair of kings), and may include a set. In any event, you are almost surely behind his entire range and should fold. But the risk is that you won't see it like that – and will just "figure" you've got to stay for his bet since you were the pre-flop aggressor.

Good and Bad Boards for C-bets

Bad Boards
In general, you want to avoid making a c-bet on what is considered a "wet" board. A "wet" board, as opposed to a "dry" board, is one that is rich in possibilities for making straights or flushes, or draws to straights and flushes. Specifically, a wet board will generally have either two or three consecutive cards, two or three suited cards, or a combination of straight and flush possibilities – something like J♥-10♥-9♠. A dry board is one without many straight or flush possibilities. A♦-8♠-4♣ is a dry board.

Good Boards
In general, you can try a c-bet on a dry board with a scare card – typically an ace or a king. When you are perceived as a generally tight player, when you raise pre-flop, your opponents will tend to put you on a range that includes premium pairs, two big cards, or a suited ace. Boards with an ace or king are especially good because your bet on the flop will tend to indicate to your opponent that you are either continuing to bet your premium pair or you have now hit top pair. They will assume that you are far ahead of them and they will tend to fold.

Rules of Thumb for C-betting

Here are some general rules of thumb when considering a c-bet, helping you avoid c-betting too frequently, and helping you size your c-bet.

- ♠ Do not c-bet all the time.

- ♠ Respect the raises of your opponents after you c-bet.

- ♠ Tend to fold rather than c-bet, when you are pre-empted by a bet on the flop.

- ♠ Don't bet more or less when you c-bet as a bluff than you do when you value bet.

- ♠ Don't c-bet as a bluff if you think your opponent(s) won't fold their hand when you bet. This sometimes (but not always) means not c-betting into more than one opponent.

- ♠ Don't c-bet as a bluff against a very short stack. He will probably figure he is pot committed and just fling his chips in out of resignation.

Seven Characteristics of Hands that Invite a C-bet

- ♠ You have position on your opponent.

- ♠ The flop has a high card and is otherwise not coordinated.

- ♠ Generally speaking, you want what is called a "dry" board.

- ♠ Your opponent isn't very deceptive.

- ♠ You have a straightforward, tight-aggressive image.

- ♠ You have not been very active lately (last ten hands).

- ♠ You have only one opponent on the flop.

- ♠ Your hand has something else of value going for it (for example a back door flush or straight, a small pair).

Seven Hand Characteristics that Should Discourage C-betting

- ♠ Your opponent has position on you.
- ♠ The hand is multi-way.
- ♠ Your opponent is very deceptive.
- ♠ Your opponent is extremely loose.
- ♠ Your opponent has a very small stack (especially if he started with a large one).
- ♠ You have been very active lately.
- ♠ You have been caught bluffing lately.

Exercise 13

C-betting

1) You have K♥-10♥ and raise to 5BB in late position pre-flop. The BTN calls, BB calls, LJ calls. The flop is A♥-7♠-6♣ and is checked to you. You want to make a c-bet. What, if anything, do you bet?
a) 25BB.
b) 30BB.
c) 6BB.
d) 12BB.

2) You have J♠-10♠ in the CO. One player calls the BB ahead of you. You raise to 3BB and have one opponent left after the K♠-8♣-8♥ flop.
   Your opponent checks. You want to make a c-bet. What do you bet?

a) 1BB.
b) 5BB.
c) 10BB.
d) 20BB.

3) You've been betting a lot lately, having had some very strong hands. You've won by betting them on the flop. Now you have Q♥-J♥ in the CO. Three players call the BB and you make it 6BB. You get a call from the BTN, the BB and UTG+3.

The flop is 10♠-8♦-8♠. The BB bets 24BB. UTG+3 folds. What do you do?

a) Fold.
b) Make it 50BB.
c) Make it 75BB.
d) Call.

Answers to Exercise 13

1) The answer is d) 12BB. The pot is 21BB on the flop. Your c-bet should be a little more than half the pot. 12BB satisfies that requirement.

2) The best answer is b) 5BB.

3) The answer is a) Fold. You have an aggressive image, your opponent bets before you act, indicating strength. You don't have a hand. Sometimes you have to accept you are beaten and lose the minimum.

How Often Should Your C-bet Succeed?

Consider the math of your c-bet. How often does your c-bet have to succeed for it to be justified?

If you are betting a little more than half pot, then the c-bet has to succeed only a little more than one time in three to show a profit.

Ironically, while you generally don't want to fire a c-bet into a multi-way pot, sometimes the size of the pot provides an especially inviting target for your c-bet. Consider this example.

> You are in the CO with A♥-Q♥. You have not voluntarily
> entered a hand for nearly two orbits, and are otherwise
> known as being a tight player. Six players call the $2.
> None of them is particularly tricky. They all seem to be on
> auto-pilot at 8:30 a.m. on a Sunday morning. You raise to
> $15. The BTN folds, and five players call your raise. With
> the dead money and the calls, there is $102 in the pot.
> The flop is K♦-6♠-3♥. The pot is checked to you. How
> often does a $55 c-bet have to win to be profitable?

♠ Half the time.

♠ Nearly all the time.

♠ 75% of the time.

♠ 33% of the time.

The answer is 33%, just about one third of the time.

I've played in many games where such a raise would succeed more
than half the time. So if the game conditions are completely favorable, it
makes sense to fire into a multi-way pot.

Here are some more examples.

> You are BTN with A♥-J♥. There are three calls before the
> action gets to you. You raise to $15. Two players call your
> raise making the pot $50. The flop is Q♠-8♥-6♦.
> Should you make a c-bet of $30 if you think there's a
> 50 percent chance they'll both fold?

Yes. If you win half the time for a $30 bet, your bet will be profitable.
For every two times you do this you'll lose $30 once and win $50 once
for a +EV of $10 per hand. (And that doesn't take into consideration the

number of times you'll win even if they call. We'll address that further under "semi-bluffing" in the chapter on deception).

Conclusion: C-bets

C-bets work. You will use them because they do. But you should also realize that your better opponents will be using them too. While you are developing your skills at defining the type of opponent you face, and while you are still working on putting your opponent on a range of hands, I suggest that you allow your opponent's c-bets to work against you. Eventually you will learn to detect them – and to take countermeasures against them. But for now, assume when your opponent raises pre-flop and then bets the flop that they have a strong range. And if your hand has not significantly improved, be ready to concede.

Chapter Four

Key Concepts:
Position, Odds and Outs

Rote memorization may work well in helping develop a rudimentary strategy for beating the game, but it's no substitute for the critical thinking necessary to develop as a winning player. In this chapter we will look at three underlying concepts in poker that are essential for you to understand how best to implement winning play.

What you'll learn: The importance of table position and the essential math that is necessary to make the right strategy decisions.

Why it's important: Winning poker depends upon analyzing specific situations and coming up with a game-plan that takes into account all the many variables. Understanding how position affects decision-making is crucial, as is the ability to make simple calculations. This chapter helps you assess the correct betting action in different situations.

Position

We looked briefly in previous chapters at how your pre-flop action is affected by your position at the table. Here we will examine the importance of table position in more depth.

General Principles of Position

Later position is favorable. All other things being equal, you want to be in last position. This is true for a few reasons. Let's list them:

Late Position Advantages

♠ You get to see the action of your opponent before you act.

♠ Your opponent has to act before seeing your action.

♠ You get to see your opponent's action before you commit any money to the pot.

♠ You get to see how your opponent reacts to seeing his cards before your reaction is known.

♠ You will see the size of the pot after your opponent bets or checks, allowing you to better gauge your pot odds than in early position.

♠ You have an opportunity to end the betting by calling or checking.

For the most part, early position puts you at a strategic disadvantage. Let's review why this is so.

Disadvantages of Being in Early Position

♠ Your opponent gets to see how you act before he has to act.

♠ You are acting before seeing how your opponent acts.

♠ Unless you go all-in or bet more than your opponent has on the table, any bet you make may be raised by your opponent.

♠ You cannot close the betting. No matter what you do, unless you go all-in or your bet has your opponent covered, your opponent may raise you.

Conclusion

As we saw earlier, you usually must play a stronger range of hands from early position than from late position. The closer to the button you are, the broader a range you can play, with the button able to play the broadest range of all. Similarly, after the flop, it is a big advantage to have position on an opponent or opponents, as you will be able to see how they act before you have to decide to act. Recognize that your position affects your tactics and your opponent's tactics – and plan them accordingly.

Exercise 14

Pre-flop

Write down the range of hands you would raise with on the button, with no calls from your opponents. Then write down the range of hands you would raise with under the gun. (Note: We covered this in Chapter 2.)

Flop

Imagine you have a pair of queens and the flop is A♥-10♥-2♣. Think about how you might play this hand differently post-flop if you:

    a) Were under the gun, raised, and were called on the button, or

    b) Were on the button, raised, and were called by a player under the gun, who checked to you on the flop.

Turn and River

This time you have A♠-K♣ and are under the gun. You called pre-flop, then called when the player on the button raised. The flop is A♦-10♦-3♥. You bet the flop with top pair, top kicker. Your opponent called.

    The 5♦ came on the turn. What would you do?

    Think about how this hand would play out if you were second to act after the flop and turn. How would things change? What position would you rather be in? Why would you rather be there?

What are the strategic considerations when you are first to act? What are the strategic considerations when you act second and have position on your opponent?

Let's say the river is the 10♥, making the board A♦-10♦-3♥-5♦-10♥. Go through the same exercise you went through for the turn. How are things different if you have early position rather than late position? Where would you rather be? Why would you rather be there?

Can you see why it is so advantageous to have position on your opponent?

Exercise 15

1) Give three reasons why early position is disadvantageous.

2) Give three reasons why late position is advantageous.

3) In general, when you are in middle position, can you play more or fewer hands than when you are in late position?

Poker Math

You must master simple poker math if you are to become a winning player. But don't be too concerned. Though it's essential, it is also very basic.

You don't need to know much math to be a good poker player. But you need to know enough to understand exactly what makes a good bet and a bad bet.

Calculating Good Bets and Bad Bets +EV and –EV

You need to understand "EV" (Expected Value) – what it is, how you calculate it, and how you rely on it to determine how you play your hand.

Simply put, a good bet is +EV and a bad bet is –EV.

"EV" stands for "expected value". Think of it as the amount of money your bet will return to you, on average, if you made it time and again, in the exact same circumstances, over an infinite period of time. If a bet is a good bet it will have a +EV. If it is a bad bet it will have −EV. Every bet can be defined in this way: +EV or −EV.

Consider this simple example that does not involve poker. Someone is flipping a fair, two-sided coin. You bet that the next flip will be heads. You are told that if you guess correctly you will be paid $10. And if you guess incorrectly you must pay $10. That is an even bet. There is neither a positive nor negative EV. The odds are exactly even that the coin will be heads as tails. You will lose exactly the same when it is tails as you will win when it is heads.

Now imagine that you have convinced someone to make the following bet. Every time you guess correctly you will be paid $20. Every time you guess incorrectly you must pay $10. That's clearly a good bet for you and a bad bet for him. Assuming a fair coin, you will still win 50 percent of the time and lose 50 percent of the time. But you will win $20 when you win and lose only $10 when you lose. On average, for every two times you flip the coin you will be ahead $10. When you average out the two flips, you are ahead $5 a flip. That would be a +$5 EV.

Again, just think of EV as a simple expression of how much you are likely to win or lose per bet, over time.

Recognize that you will not win $5 on every bet you make. In fact, you won't win $5 on any individual bet. You will lose $10 when you lose and win $20 when you win. You may, in fact, suffer many $10 losses in a row before you win your first $20. But, on average, over time, you will win $5 per bet.

Applying EV to Poker
Poker is more complicated that a simple coin flip. But the principle of EV is exactly the same. You want to make bets in poker that are +EV. Generally speaking, there are two ways to do this.

♠ You get your opponent(s) to accept bets with you that are −EV for him. The more bets and the more negative the EV the better.

♠ You avoid bets that are −EV for you.

In poker, you make a good bet if you will average making more money from your bet than you will lose. To figure that out you need to know two things. As in the coin flipping example, you need to know how much you will make when you win your bet compared with how much you will lose when you lose. That ratio of how much you win when you win to how much you lose when you lose is called "pot odds". (We touched on pot odds in a previous chapter.) We will see below exactly how to figure out your pot odds.

After you calculate your pot odds, you need to know how often, on average, you will win your bet. Those are called your "drawing odds". We will see below exactly how to figure out your drawing odds.

Whenever the pot odds are better than the drawing odds you have a good bet in poker. It is +EV. It's as simple as that.

Pot Odds

We touched on the subject of pot odds in the previous chapter, but it's important enough to return to again.

In its most simple terms, pot odds describe the ratio of money in the pot to the money you must add to call a bet. For example, if there is $100 in the pot and your opponent makes a $50 bet, making the pot $150, then the pot odds you are getting for calling that bet are 3-to-1. Compare the $150 in the pot to your $50 for the call. The ratio is 3-to-1.

Similarly, if there were $10 in the pot and your opponent bet another $10 then you would be getting 2-to-1 pot odds for your call. Compare the pot of $20 to your call of $10. The ratio is 2-to-1.

Here's another example. If there's $30 in the pot and your opponent makes a $20 bet you're getting ... do the math. Take the total of $50 in the pot and divide by the bet of $20 you must call. 50/20 = 2.5-to-1. Simple, yes?

Exercise 16

Pot Odds

Try to figure out the pot odds in the examples below.

1) You are on the button. Two players called the $2 BB pre-flop. You did as well. The SB called and the BB checked. $10 in the pot. There was a flop. SB checked. BB checked. The next player bet $10. The other player called and the action got to you on the BTN. What are your pot odds?

2) Here's a slightly more complicated exercise. Figure out your pot odds.

Pre-flop you are UTG+2. UTG folds. UTG+1 calls. You call the $2 BB as well. LJ calls. HJ raises to $15 everyone folds back to you. You call $15 and LJ calls $15.

There's a flop. You check. LJ bets $25. HJ raises to $75. Your action. What are the pot odds?

Here are some simplified exercises to make sure you are calculating pot odds correctly. In each case calculate the pot odds you're getting:

3) Pot is $120. Opponent bets $80.
   a) 2-to-1.
   b) 3-to-1.
   c) 1-to-1.
   d) 5-to-2.

4. Pot is $40. It's heads up. Hero is in early position and bets $20. Villain raises to $60.
   a) 2-to-1.
   b) 3-to-1.
   c) 4-to-1.
   d) 5-to-1.

5. Pot is $72. One opponent bets $30. Three opponents call.
   a) 4-to-1.
   b) 13-to-2.
   c) 9-to-2.
   d) 5-to-3.

6. Pot is $60. One opponent bets $40. You only have $20 left.
   a) 3-to-1.
   b) 5-to-2.
   c) 5-to-1.
   d) 4-to-1.

Answers to Exercise 16

1) There was $10 in the pot pre-flop. There was a bet of $10 and two $10 calls. That's $40 in the pot. $10 for you to call. $40 to $10 is 4-to-1. The answer is 4-to-1.

2) First add up the pot pre-flop:

Dead money: SB $1 BB $2 UTG $2 = $5

Three $15 bets = $45

Total: $50 pre-flop

On the flop there's a $25 bet and a raise to $75. That's $100 more in the pot for a total pot size of $150. You have to call $75 to stay in. $150 to $75 is 2-to-1.

3) Answer is d) 5-to-2. Pot size is $200 ($120 + $80). To call is $80. Ratio is 200-to-80 or 5-to-2 simplified.

4) Answer is b) 3-to-1. Pot size is $120 ($40 + $20 + $60 = $120). Call is $40. Ratio is $120-to-40 or 3-to-1.

5) Answer is b) 13-to-2. Pot is $192. Bet to call is $30. Ratio is $192 to $30 or, simplified 6.4-to-1 or roughly, 13-to-2.

6) Answer is d) 4-to-1.

Pot is $80 ($60 + $20, the amount of your opponent's bet that you have left).

You're now an expert on figuring out pot odds. But you don't yet know enough to figure out whether a bet is +EV or −EV. The next step is to compare your pot odds to your drawing odds. And for that, you'll need to learn first about calculating your "outs" and then more about what drawing odds are.

Outs

Put simply, an "out" is a card that improves your hand and, usually, makes your hand into a winner. For instance, if you're on a flush draw on the flop, the cards that turn your draw into a flush are called your "outs".

It's worth examining this example closely: If you have a flush draw, with two cards of a suit in your hand and two on the board, that leaves nine cards that will give you a flush. You are said to have nine "outs".

Similarly, if you have flopped a gutshot straight draw and are looking to improve to the straight, there are four cards that will help you. You're said to have four "outs".

Sometimes, you may be drawing to a few different hands that might give you a winner. Let's say you have put your opponent on a medium or low pair. You have the Q♥-J♥ with a board of K♥-10♥-2♠. Your outs are as follows.

- ♠ Nine outs for your flush – all the remaining hearts.

- ♠ Six outs for your straight – any nine or ace (yes, there are eight cards that would give you the straight, but two of those cards would also give you a flush, and we've already counted them).

- ♠ Three jacks.

- ♠ Three queens.

Presuming you're right that your opponent holds a medium or low pair, any of the above cards turn your hand into a winner. Add them all together. That's a total of 21 outs.

Exercise 17

Calculating Outs

How many outs do you have in the following examples?

1) You have J♦-J♥ and the board is 10♠-2♦-2♠-A♠. You figure your opponent has just hit his flush and you'll need to hit a jack or a deuce to win. How many outs do you have?
   a) Six.
   b) One.
   c) Two.
   d) Four.

2) You have Q♥-10♥. The flop is K♥-J♠-3♦-6♣. You figure you'll need to hit your straight to win. How many outs do you have?
   a) Two.
   b) 17.
   c) Eight.
   d) Nine.

3) You have A♠-10♠. The flop is 9♥-8♠-2♠. The turn is the K♦. You figure you'll need a flush to win. How many outs do you have?
   a) Nine.
   b) 15.
   c) Four.
   d) 13.

4) It's the river. You have K♠-K♦. The flop is K♣-J♥-10♠. The turn is 10♦. The river is the 10♣. You are sure your opponent has a 10 in his hand. How many outs do you have?
   a) Zero.
   b) Two.
   c) Four.
   d) One.

Answers to Exercise 17

1) d) You have four outs – the two jacks or the two deuces that remain.

2) c) Eight outs – the four unseen aces and four unseen nines.

3) a) Nine. There are nine unseen spades.

4) The answer is a) zero. It is the river, so there are no cards to come. With no cards to come you have zero outs. (Just seeing if you were paying attention!)

Drawing Odds

Drawing odds are the odds that you will hit the card or cards required to make your hand – usually expressed as the odds *against* making the hand.

This is best illustrated by my means of an example:

> If you have two spades in your hand, and there is one spade on the flop and one more on the turn, you can say you have four cards to a flush. You also have the river yet to appear.

You want to figure out what are the chances of you making your flush. In other words, you want to figure out your drawing odds.

You calculate your drawing odds by dividing the total number of cards you have not yet seen by the total number of cards remaining that make your hand, your "outs", described above.

In this example, 46 cards remain unseen by you, nine of which – all the remaining spades – make your flush. So we now divide 46 by nine to give 5.111. You would make your flush one in 5.111 times.

This can be expressed as a percentage as well. With one card to come, you will make your flush roughly 19 percent of the time.

You typically need to calculate your drawing odds on the flop or on the turn, and a number of similar situations occur repeatedly. For this reason, it's worthwhile remembering a few of the most common situations, and the drawing odds that apply. Here are a selection of the most common:

Hand on Flop	Final Hand	By Turn	By River
4-flush	Flush	19% / 4.2-to-1	35% / 1.9-to-1
4-straight*	Straight	17% / 4.9-to-1	32% / 2.1-to-1
4-straight†	Straight	9% / 11-to-1	17% / 5.1-to-1
Trips	Full-House	15% / 5.7-to-1	33% / 2-to-1
Two pair	Full-House	9% / 11-to-1	17% / 5.1-to-1
Two over-cards	Pair	13% / 6.8-to-1	24% / 3.2-to-1

* open-ended
† gutshot

Exercise 18

Drawing Odds

What are the odds of hitting the following draws? Consult the chart above for help.

1) You have Q♥-J♥. The board is A♥-6♥-5♠-2♠. What are the odds you'll make your flush on the river? (4.2-to-1)

2) You have A♣-A♠. The board is A♦-6♦-5♦ . You're convinced your opponent has the flush. What are the odds you'll draw the full house or better on the next card? (11-to-1) By the river? (5.1-to-1)

3) It is the turn. You have K♠-10♠. The board is A♥-K♦-10♥-6♥. You're convinced your opponent has the straight or the flush and you're trying to decide whether to call his bet. What are the odds you'll hit your full house? (11-to-1)

Try the next ones without looking at the chart.

4) It's the flop. You have Q♥-J♥. The flop is A♥-6♦-5♥. You figure you're up against a pair of aces. You want to know roughly what are the odds against you hitting the flush by the river.

    a) 5-to-1 against you.
    b) 4-to-1 against you.
    c) 3-to-1 against you.
    d) 2-to-1 against you.

5) You have A♥-K♦ and there are three low cards on the flop. Your opponent bet pre-flop and again on the flop but you think he has nothing more than a medium or small pair. You're convinced that you'll win if you hit a pair. What are your drawing odds (rounded to nearest whole number) against hitting a pair on the turn?

    a) 8-to-1 against you.
    b) 4-to-1 against you.
    c) 7-to-1 against you.
    d) 10-to-1 against you.

6) It's the flop. What percentage of the time will you hit your gutshot straight draw by the river (rounded to the nearest 5 percent)

    a) 5.
    b) 10.
    c) 15.
    d) 20.

Answers to Exercise 18

    4) The answer is d) 2-to-1 against you making the flush.
    5) The answer is c). You're a 6.8-to-1 shot to hit this one, so 7-to-1 is close enough.
    6) The answer is c).

The Two and Four Method

There's a useful shortcut for helping you figure out your drawing odds. It's called the "two and four method" and it first involves counting your "outs". To understand it, you first need to know what an out is, so refresh your memory in the section above.

Now that you understand how to *count* outs, let's apply this knowledge to help figure out your probability of improving your hand. It's simple and easy, and takes us back to the "Two and Four Method".

Instead of having to do complicated division at the tables, this shortcut gets you a good rough idea of your drawing odds by doing a very simple calculation in your head. It's a two-step process.

Firstly, count your outs as described above. Secondly, multiply your outs by two to find out the percentage chance of you hitting your hand on the *next* card.

It's called the "two and four" method because if you do this on the flop, you have two chances to hit – i.e., on the turn and the river. So you multiply your outs by four to find out the percentage of the time you're likely to hit your hand at some point over the next two cards. Examples:

> You're on a flush draw on the flop. You want to know what percentage of the time you'll hit your flush on the turn.

Count your outs. There are 13 cards of your suit, minus the two in your hand and the two on the flop leaves you with nine cards that will give you a flush. That's nine outs. Multiply that by two to find out the percentage of the time you'll hit your hand on the next card. It's roughly 18 percent.

> You're on a flush draw on the flop. You want to know what percentage of the time you'll hit your flush by the river.

Count your outs. That's nine. Multiply by four. There's roughly a 36 percent chance you'll hit your flush by the river.

These odds are not exact, but they're close enough to assist you in making your decision of whether you have sufficient drawing odds to call a bet.

Here's a more complicated example.

> You're in a moderately loose-passive $1/2 game with a $300 effective stack. You have A♥-K♥. You are in the cutoff. Only the player in the LJ called. The flop is J♠-10♥-9♥. Your opponent bets $20. You're pondering a call. What percentage of the time will you hit a straight or flush by the river?

You first need to figure out your outs. There are 12: nine cards make the flush and then three more for the gutshot straight (four queens minus the one suited queen you've already accounted for).

Quickly employ the two and four method for figuring the percentage of times you'll hit your hand. Since you have two cards to come, multiply the 12 by four. That's 48 percent.

Exercise 19

The Two and Four Method
1) You have 7♠-7♥ with the board showing K♥-J♠-8♥-6♦ on the turn. What percentage of the time will you hit a set?
   a) 2.
   b) 4.
   c) 6.
   d) 8.

2) You have 7♠-7♥ on the flop with the board showing 8♠-9♣-6♦. You figure you'll need at least a set to win. You'll hit a winning hand by the river what percentage of the time?

   a) 4.

   b) 8.

   c) 16.

   d) 40.

3) You have A♥-J♥ and are on the turn with the board showing K♦-10♥-8♠-2♥. You think your opponent has a small pair. What percentage of the time do you hit your winning hand?

   a) 9.

   b) 16.

   c) 18.

   d) 36.

4) You have 8♦-8♠ and are on the turn with the board showing 8♥-5♦-2♣-2♠. You've put your opponent on a pocket pair, anywhere from nines upward. What percentage of the time should you win the contest?

   a) 40.

   b) 76.

   c) 96.

   d) Impossible to know from information provided.

Answers to Exercise 19

   1) b) 4: You have two outs. One card to come. 2x2=4.

   2) d) 40: You have 10 outs – two for the set and eight more for the straight (four fives and four 10♠). You have the turn and the river to hit your hand. So multiply 10x4.

   3) d) 36: What do you need to win? A flush, a straight, or a pair of aces or jacks. Count your outs: nine cards make the flush, three more make the straight, and three aces and three jacks make a bigger pair. That's a total of 18 outs. It's the turn, so only one card remaining, so multiply by two. That's 36 percent.

4) c) 96: It certainly is possible to figure out from this information. Here, you need to figure out your *opponent's* chances of winning. You are clearly ahead with top full house, and the only way your opponent can out-draw you is by hitting a higher full house. You've put him on a range of six possible pairs, but whichever pair he has, the only way he hits a higher full house is if he hits one of the two remaining cards that will give him the full house. Then you'd multiply by two. His chance of hitting is 4 percent, which means you win all the other times: 96 percent.

Beware Dirty Outs!

All of the examples above have been fairly straightforward, and have deliberately not made reference to "dirty outs". But you need to understand what a "dirty out" is in order to understand their danger.

In short, a "dirty out" is an out that will make you the hand you're drawing for but may give your opponent a better hand at the same time.

Here is an example.

> You have K♥-Q♥ in late position and are one of three players who have made it to the turn. The board is J♦-10♦-6♥-4♠.

You have eight outs that will make your straight – the four queens and four nines – but you realize that one of your opponents may be drawing to the flush.

If the Q♦ or the 9♦ hit the river, you would make your straight but probably lose to a flush. Those two cards are dirty outs. You would tend to discount them and only give yourself credit for six outs – and figure out whether a call makes sense accordingly.

+EV or −EV?

You're ready to put it all together. To determine whether you have a +EV or −EV situation you need to compare your drawing odds to your pot odds. In gambling parlance, you need to determine whether the pot is paying you enough to be worth the draw.

Here's the simplest example.

> You are on the turn. You have a flush draw, with A♥-4♥ in your hand and J♥-2♥-10♠-9♣ on the board. For purposes of this example you are certain that your opponent has hit the straight on the turn. You know that you will need a flush to win, and if you don't hit it you will lose. The pot is $200. Your opponent bets $150 – the amount you have left. Should you call the bet?

Start with the drawing odds. You know that it is roughly 4-to-1 against you hitting your flush. Put another way, you will hit it roughly 20 percent of the time.

Figure out the pot odds. You will need to call $150 to win a pot of $350 ($200 in the pot plus $150 that is bet). The pot odds you figure out by dividing the total pot you'll win, $350, by the amount you must call, $150. That comes to a little worse than 2-to-1 about 2.3-to-1.

That's not nearly 4-to-1. Your drawing odds are worse than your pot odds so the bet is a bad bet. Do not call.

Here's another example.

> You have K♥-J♠. The flop is A♠-Q♦-8♣. The turn is the 2♣. There was a lot of betting up to this point, building the pot to $500. Your opponent is short-stacked and goes all-in for $100 . Should you call the bet or fold?

The pot, after your opponent's bet, is $600. Your call is $100. That's 6-to-1 pot odds. Using the two and four method of figuring our drawing odds, you calculate that with four outs (the four 10♠) and one card to come, you have roughly an 8 percent chance of winning by drawing your straight. That's an 8 percent chance of winning versus a 92 percent chance of losing. That's roughly 11.5-to-1 against you with the pot only paying 6-to-1. That's a very bad bet for you. You should fold.

Exercise 20

Key Concepts 1

It's time to put everything you've learned above into action. Try the following exercises and check the answers. If you don't get them all right, go back to the paragraphs above, reread, and retake the test until you ace it.

1) In the following examples, you have a flush draw on the turn and are sure that if you hit your flush you will win. I've provided pot sizes and sizes of your opponent's bets.

Evaluate whether or not it makes sense for you to call the bets. Indicate "call" or "fold" for each situation.

a) $300 pot, $100 bet. f) $17.86 pot, $17.86 bet.
b) $60 pot, $10 bet. g) $444 pot, $222 bet.
c) $1,865 pot, $245 bet. h) $484 pot, $100 bet.
d) $175,000 pot, $100,000 bet. i) $1,189,567 pot, $1,000,000 bet.
e) $3.24 pot, $2.12 bet. j) $86 pot, 40 bet.

2) Not all situations are quite so simple. What if you're not drawing to a flush, but to a full house. The odds against drawing a full house with one card remaining are roughly 11 to one. Accordingly, if you are drawing to a full house, and you're sure you will win you the hand, should you draw in the following situations?

The first figure is the pot size, the second is your opponent's bet.

a) $800 pot, $200 bet. f) $4,567 pot, $400 bet.
b) $1,100 pot, $100 bet. g) $1,100 pot, $200 bet.
c) $450 pot, $30 bet. h) $1,500 pot, $220 bet.
d) $10,000 pot, $5,000 bet. i) $4,498,412 pot, $400,000 bet.
e) $10,000 pot, $500 bet. j) $6.13 pot, $1.00 bet.

Answers to Exercise 20

1) a) Fold, b) Call, c) Call, d) Fold, e) Fold, f) Fold, g) Fold, h) Call, i) Fold, j) Fold.

2) a) no, b) yes, c) yes, d) no, e) yes, f) yes, g) no, h) no, i) yes, j) no.

The concept is very simple. And in the examples I gave above, the answers are simple – if not always immediately obvious.

There's another important concept, not quite so basic as drawing odds and pot odds, that you need to at least understand when you decide whether or not to call a bet. It's the concept of implied odds.

Implied Odds

These are the pot odds with another consideration – the amount of money you may *eventually* make if you make your hand. The best way to explain this is with an example from an actual game.

Let's return to the simple flush draw.

> The pot is $300. The bet is $100. Now also imagine that your opponent who made the $100 bet has another $100 left in his stack after the $100 bet. Do you think that if you hit your flush on the river you might also win that $100?

Unless your opponent is extremely good at reading you, or you have a reputation for never bluffing, or he is extremely tight – in all likelihood if a suited card hits on the river and he checks and you bet, with a pot of $600 and only $100 to call, he will probably call. You will win not $400 when you hit but $500.

If you factor that into the equation when you consider the $100 bet on the turn, that would turn a bad call into a good call. $100 to win $500 for a 4.25-to-1 shot.

When considering whether to call a bet, it is useful to think not just about the current pot odds, but the implied odds of the pot that will be enriched by the bets that are to come as well. Take a moment to think about future rounds of betting too.

This is one of the things that separates no-limit from limit poker. It's especially obvious when looking at pre-flop betting.

> Imagine a $1/2 game with 10 players. You're on the button. Everyone calls the $2. You have K♦-2♦.
> Do you call?

On the one hand, a suited king is pretty awful. It's never listed as anything but trash. It's almost always going to be an automatic fold.

But you need some additional information before tossing it aside in this spot. What if I told you that it was a very short-stacked game, with no one having more than $30? In that instance you should probably fold it.

On the other hand, what if I told you that everyone had about $1,000? In that instance it's a pretty easy call. Let me explain why.

Hands can't be valued in a vacuum. They must be viewed in the context of how much money they can win if they win – and the chances that they will win.

In a situation like this one, where everyone has called pre-flop, there's a good chance that if the perfect flop comes out, this hand may win a bundle. Hence, the likely investment of $2, in the instance above might make sense.

Consider the first case, however. If everyone is short-stacked, with only $30 in front of them, you're probably not going to win enough to warrant the extremely long odds of hitting a flush or some other winning hand. But if players are extremely deep, you might win 500 or more times your investment of $2.

The possibility that your $2 investment will return much more in future betting rounds is an example of implied odds at work. Even though the immediate pot odds are 9-to-1, if you carry the betting to its logical conclusion, the implied odds could be 500-to-1.

This notion has the potential for getting many players into a lot of trouble. Some players throw all reason out the window in the name of "good implied odds". It is an easy substitute for wishful thinking.

When considering implied odds, you should proceed cautiously. Thinking about how much you *might* win should be tempered by thinking about what is likely. Toward this end, you need to think about a few things other than the stack size of your likely opponent(s). You need to think about four things chiefly.

Will I Have the Best Hand?

In the case above, with the second nut flush draw, you probably will. There could be another flush draw out there – with a bunch of players calling the big blind. Someone might have the ace. But, in all likelihood your king will be good. And there's a chance that the ace will flop, giving you the nuts.

Will I be Able to Fold my Hand if it is not the Best Hand?

You need to think about how easy it will be to get away from your hand if you hit it but you're beaten. In this instance, it will be pretty easy. If the board pairs, making a full house possible, and anyone shows signs of aggression, you can easily fold. If the board doesn't pair there's only one hand that can beat you (short of a straight flush).

How Much Money Will I Win if I Hit My Hand?

There's no way to be sure of this, of course. But in the instance of the second nut flush, it's quite possible that you'll win a considerable amount of money – if people are deep stacked to begin with. Another flush draw might call you down. A set will probably call you down. You might even win a considerable sum from someone hitting two pair. A lot depends on the type of players you're against in this hand, to be sure. But you can see that with everyone having huge stacks, and with so many calling the big blind, it's fairly likely that you'll make a decent amount of money if you hit your hand.

How Much of a Long-shot Are You?

There are long odds and then extremely long odds. Sometimes, even if you calculate a generous number for your implied odds, the drawing odds still don't make sense. In the instance above, for example, the odds of hitting a flush on the flop are a little less than 1 percent. But the odds of hitting a flush draw are about 11 percent. That flush draw will come in on the turn about 18 percent of the time, and by the river a little more than 33 percent of the time. All totaled, if you start with the suited king, you will either hit the flush on the flop or hit a flush draw that becomes a flush by the river better than one time in 18. So for your call pre-flop to make sense, you must figure that you will end up with at least 18 times your call of $2 - $36 or so. With huge stacks, that is highly likely. With short stacks, not so much.

Another situation where implied odds tend to indicate a call, is when you hold a suited ace, with a lot of deep stacks at the table. A suited aces is a great holding because of the chance of stacking someone with another big ace in their hand. Think about having A♦-3♦ and a board of A♣-Q♥-9♦-7♥-3♣ versus A♥-K♥. You could win a ton. And you might hit it on the flop. They're not going to suspect you of it – and they might not be able to get away from it. (Of course, there's a chance that you could be stacked if the flop contains both an ace and a king.)

But again, when considering implied odds, be careful that you're not just using it as an excuse for wishful thinking.

Exercise 21

Key concepts

Here's your chance to test everything you've learned. There was a lot to get your head around in this chapter, but these four exercises should help you figure it all out.

1) You have A♥-6♥. You're on the button. A bunch of players called the $2 BB as did you. On the flop you hit a flush draw and called a $10 bet, along with two others. On the turn, the flop bettor bets $50. One

other player calls, building the pot to $150. Do you call too? You and both of your opponents have $200 effective stacks.

2) You have J♦-10♦. The flop is A♥-6♦-2♦. That gives you a flush draw on the flop. The pot is $50 and your opponent shoves out his remaining $80. Should you call the bet?

3) You started out under the gun with A♥-A♦. You raised to $12 and got two callers. The flop was K♣-Q♦-8♣. You bet $30 and got one caller. Your caller was a player that is known as a sticky nit. He is extremely tight pre-flop but then can't fold. The turn was the A♣. You bet $50. Your sticky nit opponent, who has played two hands in the past six hours, raised you to $150. You have a $500 effective stack. Do you call?

4) You're in a very loose aggressive game. You've been winning and are feeling lucky. You have A♥-K♥ and have top two pair on the turn, with the board showing A♠-K♦-10♠-6♠. Two opponents are left and the pot is $100. You bet $50, get raised to $100 and then the last player also calls the $100. You have exactly $200 left. The other players have more. They are each excellent players. Do you call the $50 raise?

Answers to Exercise 21

1) Yes. The odds against you drawing a flush are roughly 4-to-1. The pot is laying you only 3-to-1. So on the face of it, it's a bad bet. However, you must remember the concept of implied odds. There is a very good chance that if a flush hits, you will win more money on the final betting round. Your opponents will probably check when that third suited card hits. But unless they are each extremely tight, they will have a hard time folding to a bet of $75 or so. If even one of them calls you will win not $150 but $225, paying you 4.5-to-1 for your $50 investment on the turn. That makes the call worthwhile.

2) No. You are drawing to a flush to win. You have drawing odds of roughly 2-to-1 to make it by the river. The pot is $130 ($50 plus his bet of $80). You are getting pot odds of roughly 1.6-to-1 ($130 pot to a call of $80). That's not good enough. You'd want a pot of at least $160 for your $80 call.

3) Yes. You have a set and estimate that your opponent has a flush. That means you have 10 outs to win by drawing a full house or better – the nine cards that pair the K, Q, and 8, and the one ace that gives you quads. Using the two and four method, with one card left and 10 outs, you have roughly a 20 percent chance of winning – or drawing odds of 4-to-1 against you. The pot odd is roughly $300 with $100 needed to call. That's 3-to-1 pot odds. Normally when the pot odds are lower than the drawing odds, it's a bad bet and you should fold. But this is a slightly different situation. You are against a sticky nit. If you call his $100 you will have $400 left in your stack. If you hit one of your 10 outs, you are fairly certain that your opponent will call your bet, no matter how big. You stand to win another $400. That means that your implied odds aren't the lowly 3-to-1 but rather 7-to-1. Go ahead and call.

4) No. You are facing a $300 pot and asked to call for $50. Based on the betting you are certain that at least one player has you beaten with a flush. Even so, you have outs – four outs to be exact – and may draw a full house on the river. You've been running good and are feeling lucky. No matter, with four outs and one card to come you have roughly an 8 percent chance of winning. That's roughly 12.5-to-1 against you. The pot is giving you only 6-to-1 odds ($300 for your $50 call). Even if the ace or ping pair and you win another $300 ($150 from each opponent) that's still only going to pay you 12-to-1 on your money. And don't kid yourself. Getting both excellent opponents to call your all-in bet on the river when the board pairs is highly unlikely. No matter how lucky you're feeling or how well you think you're running, the odds are the odds. It's a bad bet no matter how you slice it. Fold.

Chapter Five

Estimating Ranges:
What does Villain Have?

It's not sufficient for you to understand the absolute value of your own hand. You must be able to understand it in the context of what your opponent is likely to hold. It is not possible or practical to try to narrow this down to one specific hand. Rather, poker thinking requires that you put your opponent on a likely range of hands. In this chapter we will focus on exactly how you assess the range of hands your opponent is likely to be playing.

What you'll learn: How to best figure out your opponent's range.

Why it's important: You can exploit your opponent best when you have a good idea of what he's likely to be holding.

What is a Range?

Let's talk about ranges. What are they and how can answering that question assist you in winning more money at poker?

In short, you need to understand not only the value of your hand, but how strong it likely is relative to what your opponent or opponents might have. You must always be thinking about them too. How do you stack up against the others? Thinking only of the absolute strength of your hand – or where it is on some chart – is the wrong way to view it.

Imagine that you are dealt a pair of kings. That's a great hand – unless your opponent has a pair of aces. Then it's bad. Similarly, imagine that you only have ace-high. That's bad – unless your opponent only has king-high. Then it's good.

Gauging your opponent's likely holding will help you interpret the impact of the flop, turn, and river. You can take into consideration his betting action – using it to figure out where your hand is likely to be relative to his hand.

> For example, you almost surely have the best starting hand with K♦-K♣ pre-flop. But now imagine that you have those kings and the board looks like this: Q♥-J♥-A♠-J♦-9♥.

Further, imagine that your opponent shoves the river. How are your kings looking now?

Just to put a finer point on it, it isn't that you know specifically what your opponent has. But you have a pretty good idea of the range of hands he might have. He might have two hearts for a flush, a jack for trips, a pair of queens, aces, or nines for a full house, all of which would have you crushed. A pair of kings is always a very strong starting hand, but it's not always the case by the river.

Imagine for a moment that you could see your opponent's cards when you made your betting decision. It would be an unbeatable advantage, wouldn't it? You'd be able to regularly knock him out of the hand with a well-placed bet, knowing when he missed his draw. You'd be able to call him down when he was representing a hand he didn't have. You would be invincible.

As a practical matter, unless you're cheating, you can not know with certainty the specific hand that your opponent holds. There are just too many possibilities – even if you are a great hand reader, a master of tells, very aware of your opponents' style of play, their betting patterns, and their read of you and your betting. It's just practically impossible to narrow down your opponents' likely hands to just one.

So, rather than focusing on figuring out the specific hand your opponent holds, it makes more sense to consider a range of hands – the broad spectrum of hands that he is likely to be holding – and compare your hand to that range. That's what we mean when we talk of an opponent's "range" – and it's what thoughtful players focus on when they are deciding whether and how to play their own hand.

You need to do so as well. You need to think about your opponent's range.

Determining an Opponent's Range

Let's look at a few scenarios and attempt to figure out our opponent's range as a hand progresses. We'll look at their hands pre-flop and on the flop. I'll then give you a few problems to work out on your own.

The purpose of this analysis isn't to teach you how to respond to these specific situations. Rather, it's to encourage you to think about your hand in the context of the likely holding of your opponent.

Range Analysis: Example Hand 1

Here's a pre-flop example.

> You hold a pair of jacks in UTG+3. UTG raises to 3BB.
> What's his range? What should you do?

You know him well. He is a very tight, straightforward player who rarely gets out of line. He is known as a "rock". Though you don't know exactly what he is holding when he makes that raise, you know with near certainty his range. His range is a high pair: A-A, K-K, Q-Q, J-J. But since you have J-J, you discount that specific hand and subtract it from his range. Were he not as tight and predictable you might expand it to also include A-K. But he's a very predictable rock. So you give him credit for Q-Q+.

You combine his playing type, with his position, and his betting action, and you infer his range is Q-Q+.

That's his range: Q-Q+.

You use that range to decide on your action. Your J-J is an obvious fold, as there are no cards in his range that warrant a call or a raise from you. You are very far behind all three hands he might be playing. You don't need to know which one specifically. You're far behind all of them.

If he were a little looser, you might have given him credit for raising with A-K. But even then, your jacks are practically no favorite at all. So even in that situation, you'd surely be inclined to fold. You'd be roughly tied with the 12 combinations of A-K and woefully behind the 18 combinations of the three premium pairs. The only possible exception would be if you decided to try and steal the hand from him with a raise of your own – but in the circumstances, that would be a bluff. If he called you, you'd only have the two remaining jacks as outs to beat him. That would make you a 96 percent to 4 percent underdog to hit it by the next card.

Furthermore, you are in a bad table position. One of your other opponents might choose to get involved too and defeat your plan.

Combining all this: the vulnerability of your hand, the fact he's unlikely to fold Q-Q, K-K, or A-A to your raise, and your bad table position, you shouldn't give this notion a second thought. When you consider his range, folding is the best option.

Conclusion: Fold.

Range Analysis: Example Hand 2

Most situations are not so clear cut. Imagine a slightly different scenario.

> You are on the button with J-J. A moderately loose and aggressive player, with some bluffs in him, opens the pot by raising to 4BB in the hijack seat, after everyone has folded. What's his range? What do you do?

As a loose aggressive player, in late position, he would have a much broader range than the tight competitor in the first example. This player in the HJ might be raising with any number of possible hands: medium pairs or better, middle suited connectors or better, big unsuited connectors, any two Broadway (10♠ or higher) cards, and maybe even any suited ace. Written in the range shorthand it would be: 7-7+, 10-9s+, A-10+, K-10+, Q-10+, A-2s+.

Considering your opponent's broad range, you should surely not fold your J-J on the button. Your J-J is far ahead of most of his range – all the non-pair combinations with one or both cards jacks or lower. You are a slight favorite against the three combinations of Broadway over-cards (A-K, A-Q, K-Q). You are only significantly behind the three higher pairs.

Accordingly, if he made this pre-flop move on you, your best course of action would probably be to raise him back (known generally as "three-bet").

Conclusion: Raise (three-bet).

Narrowing a Range

Range Analysis on the Flop

Ranges are not static throughout the hand. They exist for one betting round only. Once there is a flop, a turn, or a river your assessment of an opponent's range should change based on the cards that appear and the betting action that may follow. And, of course you must take into consideration your opponent's position, the type of player he is, and the type of player he thinks you are.

Let's say you put your loose-aggressive opponent on a broad range pre-flop like the one above. The flop comes. He's someone who frequently makes continuation bets. How do you think his range would narrow?

The answer is that it probably wouldn't. Here's an example of that.

Range Analysis: Example Hand 3

Let's say, for whatever reason, you didn't raise in the example above – when you had J-J on the BTN against a loose aggressive player. You just called his pre-flop raise and you both saw a flop. The flop always forces you to re-analyze your opponent's range. In the above example, let's make a few assumptions about your opponent. He's not a rock; he's somewhat loose and aggressive; and he sees you as a very tight and conventional player. You also know that when he raises pre-flop he always, or nearly always, bets the flop. In poker-speak, he has a high continuation-betting (c-bet) frequency.

> For this example hand, let's say the flop is A♥-9♠-2♦. Your opponent makes a bet of a little more than half the pot. How do you think this changes his range? What should you do in response? Let's look at it closely.

A♥-9♠-2♦ is a very "dry" board. That is, it does not lend itself to making straights or flushes. With the single high card, it invites someone to represent that they now have a premium pair. With you perceived as a very tight and conventional player, it's an invitation to your opponent to make a c-bet. You're a lone opponent. You are seen as a tight player in this scenario. You will have a high frequency of folding to a bet.

You know in this example that your opponent frequently makes c-bets. When he bets into you, how do you think his range has changed from his pre-flop range? Looked at another way, are there any hands that you thought were in his range pre-flop that you can now take out of his range – based on the new information on the flop?

It's likely that his range hasn't changed much at all, isn't it? Given the circumstances, the c-bet is almost automatic. It would be made nearly 100 percent of the time – with the exact same range as he had pre-flop.

There's only one exception. You can probably take out exactly A-A from his range. It's highly unlikely that this player would push you to fold with a bet if he were holding top set. But aside from that, he might c-bet every single hand in this spot – meaning that he would bet the flop no matter what it was. When that's the case – with a 100 percent c-bet – you don't adjust your opponent's range one bit. You combine it with the flop to see how it stacks up against your hand.

It is the same as it was pre-flop. Since you estimated that you were far ahead pre-flop, if you find yourself on the flop against this player with the same range, you should combine it with the flop and see where he is likely to be now. The flop was: A♥-9♠-2♦.

Look at the range you put him on pre-flop: 7-7+, 10-9s+ , A-10+, K-10+, Q-10+, A-2s+. You're ahead of all of the four pairs up to 10-10. You're behind the two big pairs: Q-Q and K-K. You are ahead of the suited connectors that don't contain an ace (all but one). You're ahead of the five Broadway card combinations that don't contain an ace but behind the four that do. And you're behind the remaining suited ace combinations A-2s to A-9s. All totaled, after considering all of the factors, your J-J is quite far ahead of your opponent's range. And once again, you should raise.

Conclusion: You're ahead of his range. Raise.

Range Analysis: Example Hand 4

You and the pre-flop raiser are in the same position again – but some other factors have changed in this match up.

Imagine that you are perceived as a relatively loose player who tends to call bets on the flop. And imagine that your opponent is not very deceptive at all, and only occasionally makes a c-bet on the flop. Now imagine a flop of K♥-Q♣-6♥ – two consecutive cards and two suited cards. That's called a wet board. It's likely to help many drawing hands.

If you're facing a knowledgeable opponent, likely to weigh good and bad opportunities for c-betting, it's likely that he wouldn't routinely bet this hand unless he had something at least fairly strong. He would be concerned that you had a wide range of hands that would be helped by this board. Therefore, if he did bet, it would likely mean that his hand would tend to be limited to the higher end of his starting range. Put simply, if he bet this flop he'd be more likely to actually have something.

Looked at another way, a bet on the flop from an opponent who is more selective in his c-betting means more than a flop bet from someone who c-bets all the time. Accordingly, you should tend to narrow the range of the selective c-bettor who bets the flop, and respond more cautiously. He is being more selective and you should respond accordingly.

Go back to your opponent's pre-flop raising range from the HJ seat. We deemed it the following: 7-7+, 10-9s+ , A-10+, K-10+, Q-10+, A-2s+.

> With a flop of K♥-Q♣-6♥, how might you redefine that range when he bets the flop in the HJ seat? Keep in mind that he is a player who is not given to much deception, and you have an image of moderately loose.

Let's first look at his initial range of pairs: 7-7+. With this flop we need to eliminate from his range those lower pairs – 7-7, 8-8, 9-9, 10-10, and J-J. He should be concerned that you might have a king or queen and that you would not fold to his bet.

Similarly, though it would be possible, it's unlikely he would play a big set by betting out – preferring to slow-play that hand. So it's unlikely he's holding a pair of kings or queens either. That leaves from his initial range of pairs only A-A.

Moving on to his other hands in his pre-flop range: which unpaired hands from his pre-flop range of 10-9s+, A-10+, K-10+, Q-10+, A-2s+ is he likely to continue to bet with the K♥-Q♣-6♥ flop?

Remember, he's a fairly straightforward player, not given to betting for no reason. With that in mind, he might bet the flop if he hit a pair of kings or queens or two pair. That would include the following seven hands: A-K, A-Q, K-Q, K-J, K-10, Q-J, Q-10.

Finally, look at all of the suited aces that were in his pre-flop range. It's unlikely that this player, not very creative, not prone to c-betting, in bad position, against a relatively loose opponent would bet a no pair hand on the flop. So we'd subtract these no pair, ace-high hands from his range. Instead, we'd only put him on A-K, A-Q, and maybe A-6s as possibilities. And we've already accounted for the A-K and A-Q when we listed the hands that gave him a big pair.

This leaves us with one other possible hand in his range, the A-6s. We may retain that one because it does pair him – albeit with only a pair of sixes. Nevertheless, as he would be holding top kicker, giving him three outs to beat a pair of kings or queens, he might play it. So add it to his range.

Just to clean up that list, his betting range on this flop, in this circumstance, is now A-A, A-K, A-Q, K-Q, K-J, K-10, Q-J, Q-10, A-6s.

You've succeeded in narrowing his range. Now let's look at how it compares with your own hand.

Villain's Range Versus Your Hand

Figuring out your opponent's likely range isn't supposed to be just an academic exercise. It's meant to help you figure out how to play against your opponent. With that in mind, you need to do two things: understand how your hand's value stacks up against the villain's likely range, and then decide on your best betting action.

Let's look at the example above and see how we might best respond to his betting action. Let's recap the action and then see how we would respond to our opponent's likely action.

> We have J-J. Our opponent in the HJ raised 3BB and we called. We saw the flop heads up. The flop was:
> K♥-Q♣-6♥. Our opponent bet 4BB. What's his likely range and how do we respond?

We put our opponent on a range of: A-A, A-K, A-Q, K-Q, K-J, K-10, Q-J, Q-10, A-6s. We are significantly behind against that range. We're behind all of the hands with kings or queens. The only hand we're ahead of is the last one – the pair of sixes with the ace kicker. Clearly, though J-J seemed like a fairly good hand in absolute terms, based on the way this hand developed, we need to fold.

Conclusion: fold.

Exercise 22

Range Finding
Now it's your turn. Here are six pre-flop hand situations. You're going to indicate the likely range of your opponent at this stage. Unless stated otherwise, assume 150 BB stacks.

1) Your opponent is UTG. He raised 3BB pre-flop and you called with A♥-K♥. He is a fairly tight player. His pre-flop range is best expressed as:
    a) 2-2+, A-10+, K-9+, suited ace, suited king, K-Q, K-J, Q-J, Q-10.
    b) 2-2+, suited ace, A-K, A-Q, A-J.
    c) J-J+, A-K.
    d) A-A.

2) Your opponent is a LAG on the button. There were four callers to him. He raised 5BB. His pre-flop range is best expressed as:
    a) Q-Q+, A-K.
    b) 2-2+, A-10+, K-9+, A-2s+, K-2s+, K-Q, K-J, Q-J, Q-10.
    c) 10-10+, A-K, A-Q.
    d) A-A.

3) Your opponent is a complete nit. He plays one hand in every two or three orbits, and raises even less frequently. He is in the LJ seat. There are three callers. He raises to 5BB. His pre-flop range is best expressed as:
    a) Q-Q+, A-K, A-Q, K-Q.
    b) 2-2+, A-10+, K-9+, suited ace, suited king, K-Q, K-J, Q-J, Q-10.
    c) 10-10+, A-K, A-Q.
    d) A-A, K-K, A-Ks.

4) Your opponent is about average in tightness – maybe a little loose at times. He is only moderately aggressive. He is on the button. The pot was three-bet to 8BB and, when the action gets to him, he shoves 50BB. His likely pre-flop range is best expressed as:

a) A-A, K-K, A-Ks.
b) J-J+, A-K, A-Q, K-Q.
c) 2-2+, A-10+, K-9+, suited ace, suited king, K-Q, K-J, Q-J, Q-10.
d) 8-8+, A-K, A-Q.

5) UTG+2 and LJ called the BB. You raised to 4BB on the BTN with J-J. UTG+2 folded. The LJ, a loose-passive player – and not a very experienced or good one – called your raise. His likely pre-flop range is best expressed as:
a) J-J+, A-K, A-Q, K-Q.
b) 2-2+, A-10+, K-9+, suited ace, suited king, K-Q, K-J, Q-J, Q-8+, 9-8s+, 10-8s+, J-8s+, Q-7s+.
c) 8-8+, A-K, A-Q.
d) A-A, K-K, A-Ks.

6) You called the BB in the LJ with A-Ks, after three other players called. The LAG HJ raised 5BB and the BTN, a fairly tight and skillful player, called. You called. The BTN's likely range is best expressed as:
a) 2-2+, A-2s+, J-10s+, Q-Js K-Q, K-J, A-J+.
b) J-J+, A-2s+, J-10s+, Q-Js K-Q, K-J, A-J+.
c) 2-2 to J-J, A-2s+, J-10s+, Q-Js K-Q, K-J, A-J+.
d) A-2s+, J-10s+, Q-Js K-Q, K-J, A-J+.

Answers to Exercise 22

1) c) This is a typical raising range in early position for a relatively tight player.

2) b) The other answers are too tight for a LAG.

3) d) A nit would only raise from middle position with these extremely strong holdings.

4) a) For anyone but a maniac, a four-bet requires a very strong hand. This range expresses that narrow range.

5) b) This is the only answer that shows a broad range that a loose-passive player would likely play. The other ranges are much too narrow.

6) c) The problem with all the others is that they don't account for the fact that he called and didn't raise. By not raising, he made it unlikely that he was playing his top pairs. Though he would call with a very broad range, recognizing that the raiser was a LAG, he almost surely would have three-bet with Q-Q+, and certainly with K-K+ in order to try and isolate the LAG.

Exercise 23

Reading Opponents on the Flop
Here are a few more examples at different stages of hands. Try to figure out what you can put your opponent on.

1) Your opponent (Villain) is completely clueless – maybe never played poker before. He tends to call if it's just the BB no matter his table position or cards. He has called nearly all of the hands that haven't been raised, yet has never raised himself. Six of you called pre-flop. Villain is UTG. You are in the CO.
  Let's start right there. With what I've described of Villain's play, which of the following best describes his likely pre-flop range:
  a) Q-Q+, A-K.
  b) J-10s+, A-Q, A-K, Q-Q+.
  c) Just about anything.
  d) 2-2+, 8-9s+, A-10+.

2) The flop is A♦-J♦-6♠. The same Villain bets. Everyone folds to you. You have A♠-3♠. What is Villain's likely range?
  a) A-A.
  b) A-A, J-J, 6-6, A-2+, J-6.
  c) Just about anything.
  d) 2-2+, 8-9s, A-10+.

3) You face a very tight, aggressive, selective, tough regular. The flop is 9♦-8♥-7♠. He's UTG+3. You are the HJ. Your image is very tight. He raised 3BB pre-flop. You called. He now bets 4BB. Range?

    a) 7-7+, A-K.

    b) 2-2+, A-2s+.

    c) J-10, 6-5, J-J+, A-6, A-10.

    d) Just about anything.

4) Villain is a nitty regular. Straightforward. Untricky. Doesn't like to back down once he decides to play. You think of him as a sticky nit, but he seldom plays and rarely raises. You are the CO. He is the BTN. Three callers to you pre-flop. You raised to 3BB with A♥-Q♥. He called. UTG+2 also called. Flop is 8♠-8♥-3♥. UTG+2 checks. You c-bet 6BB. BTN makes it 15BB. UTG+2 folds. What is BTN's range?

    a) A-A.

    b) Just about anything.

    c) J-J+.

    d) J-J+, 9-8, 10-8, J-8, Q-8, K-8, A-8.

5) Villain is a somewhat drunk LAG, who is raising 75-80 percent of the unraised pots from late position, while laughing. You should have a nitty image in his mind, but you're not sure how much he's paying attention. Pre-flop, there are two callers to you. You raised to 5BB with 10-10 in UTG+3. He made it 15BB on the button. The two limpers folded. You called. The flop was A♠-9♦-3♠. You checked. He shoves for 100BB range?

    a) 2-2+, A-2s+, K-Qs, Q-Js, J-10s, K-Qo, A-J+.

    b) 2-2+, A-2s+, A-J+.

    c) J-J+, A-K, A-Js+.

    d) Just about anything.

Answers to Exercise 23

1) c) Since he calls with just about any cards, and since he called in this instance, you can't narrow down his range at all. He may have just about anything.

2) b) A clueless player knows few things about poker, but he maybe knows enough to recognize that a pair of aces or better is a good hand, worthy of a bet. While a) is a betting hand, putting an opponent on only one hand at this stage is much too narrow an assessment. There are many other hands that also might bet. b) represents the only range of hands that explains all Villain's bets, without including hands that this clueless player would never bet with.

3) a) You have to review the significant pieces of data you have: his image, your image, his position, his action pre-flop, the flop, and his flop action. He's a rock playing against a player with a tight image. He's in middle position. He will have a very narrow raising range – probably no less than a mid-pair and A-K or A-Q. There is a wet (coordinated) board with no high card. He's unlikely to be c-betting with nothing. Still he bets. You'd have to figure he started with a pair or A-K and is still betting it strongly hoping you'll fold. The range that fits that description is a). The other options are too broad to fit with his pre-flop raising range.

4) Let's consider each possibility in turn.

a) Villain may well have this hand in his range. But he probably would have raised with it pre-flop. Is it the only hand he'd raise with on the flop? No.

b) You're just giving up if you're considering this. There are far too many hands he'd never call pre-flop or raise with on the flop. Definitely not b).

c) Looks good. He might well have called pre-flop with these pairs, figuring that he'd have position on the flop and could do his raising then unless something scary came up. Raising on the flop is uncharacteristic, so it probably represents a very strong hand.

d) You might think that this makes sense, since a very tight player who rarely raises might wait until he hit trips to do any raising. But it doesn't make sense in the context of the pre-flop betting he did. As a nit, he's not calling a raise pre-flop without a strong hand – and none of those hands are sufficiently strong to warrant a call.

Best answer is c).

5) d) While we could drill down deeply into this hand and try to put him on a small range, the most important piece of information was right there at the top. His style of play is so loose and aggressive that he could have anything here – even 7-2 – if only to prove that he can win with a terrible hand.

Chapter Six

Deception: Why it is Important

In pop culture, deception is often extolled as the sin qua non of poker. In reality, its importance is often over-estimated. In this chapter we'll learn all about deceptive poker moves like bluffing , semi-bluffing, slow-playing, and trapping. But we'll also learn why it's often more important to play straightforwardly.

What You'll Learn: How best to be selectively deceptive when the situation calls for it.

Why it's important: Used correctly, and judiciously, deception can greatly enhance a good player's ability to win money.

Introduction

I meet and speak with many people who don't play poker, but who watch it on TV and in the movies. They often ask questions about playing the game. Typically, they ask three things, often in quick succession: Have I been on TV? Do I have a poker face? And do I bluff much?

Most people think that deception – and bluffing in particular – is the most important ingredient of winning poker.

Many who play in the $1/2 and $1/3 games have incorrectly embraced deception when they should have embraced solid, straightforward, largely undeceptive play.

A lot of deception is generally wrong for players in many low level games that are filled with players who lack the knowledge or self-control to fold correctly when their opponents represent superior hands with their betting. Even when the tightest player in the world raises in early position pre-flop, their opponents aren't putting them on a narrow range. They're not putting them on any range at all. They're playing to gamble, hoping they get lucky on the flop, and gladly call because it's "only $10" or "they feel lucky".

(If you doubt that players are in the poker room to gamble, just think about what all of the people outside the poker room, in the rest of a casino, are doing all the time. They are playing games that they know, with certainty, have a house advantage – and that they have no chance of winning in the long run. Why should most poker players be any different? Most are playing poker as a fun diversion, and they probably know they are losing. But they don't care. They play poker for fun – not because they think they have any real chance of gaining an edge over the other players in the game.)

When you're playing against players like that (and you should look for games where they're playing) you'd be foolish to waste a lot of clever and deceptive plays on them. Their chief flaw is that they are not folding to legitimate value bets. So why would they fold to your deceptive ones?

When you are playing in the typical $1/2 and $1/3 no limit hold'em games, rather than thinking about how to make a deceptive play, for the most part, focus on the fundamentals of straightforward play, banking on your opponents making the mistake of calling and folding incorrectly – without being fooled.

Here's an example of what I mean.

I was playing in a $1/2 game in a casino. I had watched the play of the game for a while before I sat down. It was recreational. Players were drinking, having fun, and playing very loosely. Typically, a hand would be called by nearly all the players pre-flop without a raise. Sometimes someone would raise to $8 or $10 and a few people would call. There would typically be a bet on the flop, called by a couple or three players. On the turn there might be a bet with a caller or two. And the river was often checked down – or bet and called. I don't think there was a three-bet or a check-raise the entire 20 minutes or so that I watched.

Players would call with lots of hands that a very good player would never play.

One hand in particular ended up a contest between two players as follows:

CO: A serious and regular player with a generally sour demeanor. He had just recently sat down. We'll call him "Sour Puss".

UTG+3: Happy-go-lucky recreational player. Drinking a bit. Having fun. Playful. He seemed relatively new to casino poker. We'll call him "Happy Guy".

Effective stacks $300.

Happy Guy called the $2 BB as did a couple of others before the action got to Sour Puss. Sour Puss raised to $15. BB called. Happy Guy called. Pot $50.

Flop: A♥-7♠-6♥
BB: Check
Happy Guy: Check
Sour Puss: Bet $30
BB: Fold
Happy Guy: Call $30
Pot: $110

Turn: A♥-7♠-6♥-K♥
Happy Guy: Check
Sour Puss: Bet $80
Happy Guy: Call
Pot: $270
River: A♥-7♠-6♥-K♥-2♦

Happy Guy: Check
Sour Puss: Shoves for $175
Happy Guy: Calls $175

Sour Puss: Turns over Q-Q – with a scowl
Happy Guy: Smiles and turns over K♦-8♣

Sour Puss says loudly and very upset, "How could you call me with that shit? What did you think I had?"

Happy Guy, smiling and a bit puzzled, "I don't know. But a pair of kings is a *good* hand!"

How are you going to bluff a guy like that who isn't thinking about what you are likely to have?

(And, for the record, why would any good player berate a player who plays like that? This is exactly the type of player you want to welcome with open arms to the poker game.)

Why You *Must* Use Deception

While you're not going to focus chiefly on being deceptive, you must learn to incorporate it into your game. If not – if you only play straightforwardly, sooner or later, even your poor opponents will recognize that you only bet when you have a strong hand. When that happens – sooner with good observant opponents, later with your poor opponents – you will not be able to make much, if any, money with your good hands – as your opponents will decline to play against you. Similarly, you will not be able to make any money on your hands that aren't extremely strong, as your opponents will know that you will fold when they are aggressive – encouraging them to bet strongly against you all the time. The only time they will have to retreat is when you do indeed have a strong hand and show strength.

Imagine what it would be like to play against your opponents with their cards concealed and yours exposed. If you only play straightforwardly – never bluffing with your weak hands and never slow-playing your strong hands – it will be as if you are playing your cards face up. To avoid that, you must learn to mix up your game, incorporating elements of deception. Deception, used judiciously, will leave your opponents unable to get a clear fix on the true strength of your hands. You want your opponents to be at least slightly confused. They won't be sure how to act against you. By creating uncertainty you are increasing the chances that your opponents will make mistakes against you – mistakes that you can use to increase your profit.

Selectively Deceptive Play (Don't Try This at Home)

I saved the topic of deception until now because it is generally given too much attention, too early in a learning player's education. Against poor and mediocre opponents, it's straightforward value betting that will make you the most money. Even so, it's important for you to fully understand the concept of deception. You will use it against your better opponents. And it's helpful to understand it because many of your opponents think that this is what the game is all about.

There are, broadly speaking, two types of deception. There is deception that is designed to make your hand look stronger than it really is, with the intent of getting your opponent to fold. And there is the deception designed to make your hand look weaker than it is, with the intent of getting your opponent to call or bet into a hand that is better than theirs. The former is broadly referred to as "bluffing". The latter is broadly referred to as "trapping". We'll deal with that first type first.

Deception: Trying to Look Strong When you are Weak

Bluffing

Bluffing is an attempt to make your hand appear stronger than it truly is, by betting or raising. You do it to change the behavior of your opponent from what it would be if they knew the true weakness of your hand. Most frequently it is used to convince an opponent to fold a hand that is stronger than yours, convinced by your betting action that your hand is stronger than it truly is.

Here is an example of a simple bluff. All examples are from a $1/2 no-limit game.

Villain: (x–x)
You: (A♠-Q♥)
Board: K♠-J♠-9♥-6♦-5♠

Villain raised to $8 pre-flop, bet $10 on the flop, and $20 on the turn. He now checks the river. The pot is $82.

You bet $40 on the river with your unpaired A-Q hoping to get your opponent to fold by convincing him that you just hit a flush, and winning you the $82 pot.

That's a bluff. You have ace-high, against what you presume to be a better hand. You want to convince Villain that you were calling along with a spade flush draw that you just hit with the 5♠. If your opponent folds, your bluff was successful. If he calls or raises your bluff failed.

You would judge your $40 bluff to be a successful tactic in the long run if you succeeded with it at least a third of the time. You'd lose $40 twice (a total of $80), but win once for $82 – a profit of $2 every three hands on average – or $.66 per hand. If you succeeded with it half the time, it would show a bigger profit. You'd lose $40 once and win $82 once, for a profit of $42, or $21 per hand.

Not all bluffs occur on the river. You could make a bluff pre-flop and on all other betting rounds. Here's an example of a pre-flop bluff. It is a $1/2 game and everyone folds to the cutoff who opens for $15. You are on the button with J♠-9♠ and re-raise to $35. Here you are re-raising with a speculative hand that you doubt is stronger than the hand of your raising opponent. But you want him to fold.

You can imagine bluffs in many other situations.

Bluffing on Two Rounds of Betting

You might use more than one betting round to fully execute your bluff. Imagine the example above. Instead of folding to your raise, your opponent calls. Therefore, there is $73 in the pot and the flop is: K♠-7♣-4♦. You are playing with effective stacks of $200.

Your opponent, Orno, has first action and you act after he does.

Recalling your raise before the flop, Orno checks. It's a dry flop. There are no serious straight or flush possibilities for someone who raised and then called your three-bet. The flop hasn't hit you – except with a back-door spade flush draw (you have to hit two spades for a flush). Nevertheless, you decide to continue to represent strength by betting $45. Orno folds.

That would be a successful bluff as well. You initiated it pre-flop and then finished it on the flop. You can imagine that such a tactic could also continue to the turn and even the river. They're all bluffs – relying on your hand appearing to be stronger than it is.

I mentioned that this was a simple bluff. (This is also known as a "naked bluff"). That doesn't mean that it was easy or simple to execute. It may have been hard for you to do. The term "simple bluff" means that it was the kind of bet that only works if your opponent folds. As such, you would measure its success strictly by whether it accomplished the task of winning the pot by getting your opponent(s) to fold. In the latter example, your bluff would fail if anyone called.

Semi-bluffing

Not all bluffs are simple bluffs. There are often some other complexities that make bluffing fit other purposes as well.

For example, suppose when you bet as a bluff, you had another way to win other than by getting your opponent to fold. Imagine you had a backup plan to go with your bluff – a way that you could win even if your opponent called your bet.

We call bets like these – bluffs with back up plans – "semi-bluffs".

Here's an example of a semi-bluff.

> You have K♥-10♥ with a board of A♥-7♥-6♠-9♣ on the turn. Your opponent has been leading the betting on each betting round. You have been calling. Once again your opponent bets. You raise. That would be a semi-bluff.

You have two ways to win with this bet. First of all, your raise might convince your opponent to fold – fearing that it indicates you just hit a straight. You would win as a bluff. But if he doesn't fold you still have nine outs to hit the nut flush on the river. As you can see, it's impossible to semi-bluff on the river. There are no more cards to come so there is no way to improve. Your bluff either works or doesn't work.

Similarly, it isn't a semi-bluff if there isn't at least some chance that your bet will induce a fold. It wouldn't be a semi-bluff if you assumed your opponent would call you. That would just be betting on the come – anticipating that you might improve on the next card.

When figuring out whether a semi-bluff makes sense you must first estimate its *full* chance of success. To do that you simply add the chances that it succeeds as a bluff to the chances of your hand improving to a winning hand on the next card.

It's easiest to put this in terms of percentages. If, for example, you estimated that you might win as a bluff half the time (50 percent), and that your hand might improve on the next card 20 percent of the time (a flush draw for example), then the total chance you might win the hand is 60 percent (50 percent plus 20 percent of the remaining 50 percent of the time – which is 10 percent). If, on the other hand, you estimated that your hand might succeed as a bluff 50 percent of the time, but you could only win if you hit a full house or better, then you'd add 50 percent not to 10 percent but to about 4 percent as you only have about an 8 percent chance of drawing the full house. (Eight percent of 50 is 4 percent.)

There's another advantage to a semi-bluff that's also worth considering. When you make your bluff, if you then catch your drawing hand it is less likely that you will be believed when you bet. So it's more likely that you can make more money on the next round of betting.

Consider the following hand.

> You're drawing to your flush. You raise your opponent's bet on the turn, representing a strong hand. He calls you. If you then hit your flush on the river and bet, he'll be less likely to think you are betting your flush, since your bet on the turn would not be the typical action of someone on a flush draw. So there's a better chance you'll be paid off.

Keep in mind that you should not semi-bluff or engage in any deceptive action habitually. It should be done sparingly. If you start doing this all the time you will end up not being believed when you bluff, and you will be much less successful at it. Better to do it occasionally and against players at least good enough to consider what it is that you are representing.

A semi-bluff does not necessarily have to include improvement, just the illusion of improvement. It may be, for example, that your semi-bluff works because the board appears to improve, causing your opponent to fold when you fire again.

Here's an example.

> Suppose you are the BB with Q♦-J♦. A player raises in late position and the button calls. You call as well. You check and the bettor bets the flop of K♠-A♠-6♦. The button folds. You raise with only straight draw. Your opponent calls. The turn is the 8♠. You bet. Your opponent folds.

You raised as a semi-bluff on the flop, representing that you had a set or top two. And when the spade came on the turn, it looked enough like you might have improved for you to get your opponent to fold when you bet again. It too is a semi-bluff.

As you can see, a semi-bluff is more likely to succeed than just a bluff. It is a bluff with a back-up plan.

Semi-demi-bluffing

A semi-demi-bluff is a semi-bluff that is also a value bet. Here's an example of such a bet.

> You hold J♥-10♥ on the BTN. A LAG raises to $10 from the CO. You call. The flop is A♥-10♠-6♥. Villain bets $15. You raise to $45. That's a semi-demi-bluff.

It's a semi-bluff, since you are raising with the hope that your opponent will fold what is likely to be a better hand – the ace – while you also have the possibility of improving to a flush on the next card. But it's also a possible value bet because your pair of 10♠ may actually be the better hand. Villain may just be c-betting without having hit anything.

Consider three ingredients when contemplating a semi-demi-bluff.

- ♠ What is the probability that my bet will succeed as a bluff?

- ♠ What is the probability that my bet will succeed by improving or seeming to improve on the next card?

- ♠ What is the probability that my hand is the best hand at the moment?

The addition of values may make a semi-demi-bluff worthwhile, when it wouldn't otherwise be.

Let's say it is the turn. You have J♥-10♥. The board is 10♠-9♥-8♠-8♣. You are in late position and it is checked to you. Your bet might take the pot away from your opponent. You may improve to the best hand on the next card if a queen or seven hit the river. And your 10-10-8-8-J may be the best hand. Those three possibilities almost surely warrant a bet.

Exercise 24

Betting to Look Strong as a Bluff

Below are five different scenarios. Read them all carefully. Identify what type of bet you are making in each case. Choose from bluff, semi-bluff, semi-demi bluff, then explain what needs to happen for you to be successful.

1) Pre-flop: In the CO. You have K♠-Q♠. Everyone folds to the HJ who raises to $10. Everyone folds to you. You raise to $25.

2) Pre-flop: In the HJ. Folded to the LJ who makes it $10. You make it $30 with A♥-J♥.

3) River: You have A♠-K♠ UTG. You bet $10 pre-flop, $25 on the flop, $50 on the turn. The board is J♠-10♠-10♥-2♦-7♦. You have two opponents. You shove for $350.

4) Turn: You have K♠-10♣. You are the BTN. UTG+1, a LAG, raised to $10 pre-flop and was called by two players. You called as well. On the flop of J♠-9♠-2♦ UTG bet $25. Only you called. On the turn of 8♣ your opponent checks. You bet $60.

5) Turn: You have A♣-4♣ in the HJ. Pre-flop: You and six others called the BB. You are in next to last position. The flop was 9♣-8♦-2♣. The SB checked, big blind checked, UTG+2 bet $10. You called and the big blind called. The 10♥ turned. UTG+2 bet $20. You raised to $50.

Answers to Exercise 24

1) You are semi-demi-bluffing. You are hoping that you can get your opponent to fold his better hand, but you might improve, and you might actually hold the better hand already.

2) Once again, you are semi-demi-bluffing. You are hoping that you can get your opponent to fold his better hand, but you might improve, and you might actually hold the better hand.

3) This is a pure bluff. There can be no semi-bluff or semi-demi bluff when there are no cards to come. To be successful you must convince your opponent to fold. With a $400 bet into a pot of roughly $175 you must be successful roughly two-thirds of the time.

4) This is a semi-bluff. You are betting with hope that you will get your opponent to fold. But if you don't succeed you have four outs – with the queen giving you a straight. A pure bluff would have to succeed 40 percent of the time to break even. You will win by improvement roughly 8 percent of the time. So for your semi-bluff to show a profit you need to win as a bluff more than 32 percent of the time. So if you gauge your chances of winning as a bluff one third of the time or better, then this move makes sense. And, since you will likely make even more money on the river if your hand is called and your draw comes in, you don't even have to succeed as a bluff quite as often as 33 percent of the time for the move to show a profit.

5) This is a semi-bluff. You are hoping your raise will succeed. But if it doesn't you may hit a flush on the river. Your bluff alone works if you succeed about half the time. But your hand may improve on the river about 20 percent of the time. So your bluff really only needs to succeed about 30 percent of the time for this semi-bluff to make sense. And, as in the example above, you may also win additional money on the river when hit your hand. So you don't even need the full 30 percent success rate on your bluff for the move to show a profit.

Deception – Acting Weak When You're Strong

Deception is not just about appearing strong when you're weak. It may also be an attempt to appear weak when you are strong. There are generally two ways this is done – each with a different purpose.

Check-raising

Check-raising involves three betting actions – two from you and one from an opponent. It can only be performed on the flop, turn, or river.

The first part of the act involves a player who has been dealt a strong hand. He checks with the expectation that his opponent will bet and with his intention of raising that bet. In this way he hopes to extract extra money from his opponent – money that he would not have gained had he bet his hand conventionally, by betting it at first without checking.

Here's an example of a check raise.

> You hold 9♥-9♦. You are in early position, call the big
> blind, and call the raise to $12 of the player on the button.
> All other players fold. The flop is A♠-K♠-9♥. You check,
> hoping your opponent bets so you can raise. Sure enough,
> he bets $15. You raise to $30. That's a check-raise.

You're happy if your opponent calls you, as you figure to be
in the lead. You're happy to win the pot right there so there's
no chance of him improving.

Here's another example.

> It's the river. You're in early position with K♥-K♠. You've
> been leading the betting. On the turn, the board is:
> A♥-9♥-7♠-7♥. You bet again and you're opponent
> raises. You call. The river is K♦. You check expecting
> your opponent to bet; he obliges you and bets;
> and you raise. That's a check-raise.

Players can surely debate whether those check-raises were helpful. It
may well be that betting those hands directly would have been a better
play. But the point is that it is a form of deception – looking weak with a
check, only to come out with a raise because you are really strong.

Slow-playing

The other form of deception is a slow-play. A slow-play extends the
deception into another round of betting. It is usually done only when you
are extremely strong – stronger than you'd be for a check-raise, since
you are risking the improvement that might occur on the next round of
the deal.

Here's an example of a slow-play.

> You are dealt J♥-J♦ in late position. You raise four callers to $15. Three of them call you. The flop is A♣-J♠-J♣. Your three opponents check to you. You also check.

You are checking because you have just flopped quad jacks and don't want to knock everyone out with a bet. You'd rather they improved to a hand that might be willing to give you action. That's a slow-play.

Obviously, you wouldn't use this play on the river, since that's your last opportunity to bet.

Here's another example that illustrates the risk of slow-playing hands that are strong but not incredibly strong.

> You started with A♥-A♦ in mid-position. The action came to you and you decided not to raise with your excellent hand. You only called the big blind and six players saw the flop.

The flop was 9♦-8♠-8♦. Your first opponent checked, your second opponent bet $10. You raised to $25. The next two players folded. The button raised to $60, the player who checked called as did the player behind you. Are you feeling good having checked your aces as a slow-play?

Exercise 25

Here are 10 hands. In all instances you have an effective stack of 400BB.

If the first five pre-flop situations, figure out which hands you would routinely play slowly to deceive your opponents.

1) 7-7 UTG.
2) K♥-Q♥ Button.
3) Q-Q Middle Position. One caller in front of you.
4) A♥-K♦ UTG+3.
5) A-A on the Button, Everyone Folds to You: Extremely Tight Blinds.

The next five hands are post-flop.

6) You have A♥-10♥ in late position and called a pre-flop raiser. The flop was Q♥-7♥-6♥. Your opponent bet half the pot.

7) You have A♠-5♠ in early position. You were the second limper. A later position player raised 4BB and you both called. The flop came A♥-K♦-5♥. Your first opponent checked. You hit two pair. Do you slow-play your two pair?

8) You have A♠-5♠ in late position and called a pre-flop raiser. You are now heads up on the J♠-9♠-2♠ flop. Your opponent checks. Do you check too?

9) You have 2-2 in late position. You are new to the table and unknown to the other players. An early position player raised 3BB and two opponents called before the action got to you. You called. The flop was Q♠-J♠-2♣. The pre-flop raiser bet 7BB. The second player raised to 15BB. The next player folded. Should you slow-play?

10) It's the river. You have Q♥-J♥. You are under-the-gun. Five players got to the flop having called a late position raise to 5BB. The flop was K♥-10♥-2♦. Two of you called the pre-flop raiser's bet of 15BB. The turn is the 2♥. You bet 30BB. Your opponent raised to 70BB. You called with your made flush and open-ended, two out, straight flush draw. The river was the 9♥. Do you slow-play with your straight flush?

Answers to Exercise 25

1) No. Not nearly strong enough. In fact, you might not play it at all in this position in a tight aggressive game.

2) No. While this is a hand you might call or raise with, you surely would not slow-play it to deceive your opponents into thinking you had a weak hand.

3) No once again. Q-Q is a strong hand to be sure, but pre-flop, especially with a caller, it doesn't warrant a deceptive slow-play.

4) No. Surely not. While you might want to call with A-K pre-flop, it isn't because the hand is so strong that you want to be deceptive. It's

because the hand is not yet made – and you might want to fold it on the flop if it doesn't improve.

5) Maybe. Your raise will almost surely cause the blinds to fold. But even here, since your position would tend to cause even a moderately perceptive opponent to suspect how strong you were, thinking you might just be trying to steal the blinds, a standard raise here might itself deceive your opponent into 3-betting. And wouldn't that be great?

6) Slow-play here. You want to call, not raise. A raise will often cause your opponent either to fold immediately or to check and fold the turn if he hasn't significantly improved. You'll probably make more money by letting him continue to lead the betting, with you feigning weakness.

7) Probably not. You almost surely have the best hand, but what's the advantage in deceiving your opponent here? If neither opponent has an ace, they'll probably fold (unless they think you're trying to deceive them with your aggression – and that you have nothing). If you check, the pre-flop raiser may make a c-bet without an ace, but he may also check behind you fearing a weak ace from either you or the other player. The turn may be a scary card for you – if it's a heart or a king. Best to just bet your hand.

8) Probably – but maybe not. The advantage of checking is that your opponent may improve on the next card and give you action, while he probably won't give you action when he checks and you bet the flop. Against a simple or poor player, checking might well make sense – a true slow-play. But against a player with even a little imagination, your bet might seem fishy, as he'd suspect you wouldn't bet if you actually hit the flush. Don't assume that the best way to extract value from your opponent is to slow-play. It probably is in this situation, but against the right opponent a bet might be best.

9) No. Don't slow play. Though you have a set of twos, your hand is not strong enough to stand improvement from an opponent, and the board is too wet. There are too many draws that beat you if they hit. You may even be behind another set. You are not afraid of showing strength here and should three-bet. One or even both of them might think you're

doing so on a big draw and may call you down. But if you win all 34BB right here, that's good!

10) This is a trick question. You can't slow-play on the River, you can only check-raise. Regarding the check-raise, don't go for it. There's too much chance that your opponent won't bet if you check – figuring the only hand you'll call with is a straight flush. Bet your hand, have them wonder whether you are bluffing with the obvious straight flush draw being hit. Most players at this level won't be able to fold the nut flush.

Conclusion on Slow-Playing

Beginning and intermediate players often slow-play too frequently, embracing deception when they should be embracing straightforward play. While it makes sense to mix up your play to avoid being too predictable, it does not make sense to slow-play too many hands against bad or mediocre players. Their general flaw is that they are too eager to call. Exploit that tendency by playing your strong hands strongly.

Your bet, when you are very strong, generally accomplishes three things that are all good. First, it often gets a call – making you more money than if you checked. Second, if you are called, it builds the pot for future betting rounds, making it less likely your opponents will fold to future bets, thinking they are "pot committed". And third, it makes it more likely that you will not have to show your hand. Your opponents, though they will often call you, will surely fold more than if you checked.

By not showing down the winner, you will leave your opponents guessing about what you had – adding to your ability to keep them from having a solid read on your play in the future.

Chapter Seven

Player Types: Know Your Villains

Poker players vary – in many ways. One can easily get lost in the weeds of their personal idiosyncrasies of play. More useful is to put them into broad categories or "types" so we can adjust our strategies to best take advantage of them. In this chapter we will identify the basic types of poker players and learn strategies tailored to best exploit each of them.

What you'll Learn: How to identify and exploit different types of players.

Why it's Important: When it comes to winning money from our opponents, one style of play doesn't fit all.

Introduction

Once upon a time there was a computer game. It was a poker game with about 30 different programmed poker players against whom you would play. Each was programmed to play certain hands in a certain way. "Tight Tina" would fold every single hand pre-flop unless it was a premium pair. And then she would fold that hand, to a bet on the flop, if there was even one overcard – unless she hit a set. "Loose Larry" called every bet no matter how large until it was impossible for him to improve to a winner.

The correct play against these two extreme player profiles would vary. You'd bet just about every hand against Tina, knowing that unless she held a really strong hand, she'd concede and you'd win. Similarly, you'd never try to bluff Larry, since he'd call everything. But you'd value bet him when you had a strong hand – and end up with all of his money.

Of course, in the real world, players are rarely so simplistic. Still, with even a little observation, you'll notice that players can be grouped into different categories based on their general patterns of play. By figuring out in which category they are in, you can make money from them by playing hands differently. In the broadest sense, you end up playing the player as much as you are playing your cards.

The first step toward this goal is to get in the habit of observing your opponents and putting them into different categories. I call this "typing your opponent".

Keep your designations simple and easy to remember. Use terms that make sense to you. They don't have to be my terms. But here's what I use.

You're going to keep it extremely simple to start, with a binary system. Put opponents into one of two categories, either tight or loose.

Then use another binary system. Put them into one of two other categories, either passive or aggressive.

The words mean exactly what you think they mean. A tight player plays few hands. They fold most of the time. They play a very tight range of very strong starting cards. A loose player plays a lot of hands. They call much of the time. They play a very broad range of hands that include strong and not-so strong starting cards.

A passive player plays their hands passively, with calls rather than bets or raises. An aggressive player is the opposite, tending to initiate or accelerate the betting with bets and raises and re-raises.

Now combine those characteristics. You will end up with four broad types of players: tight-aggressive, tight-passive, loose-aggressive, and loose passive.

One simple way of thinking of opponents is to plot them on a graph. One axis represents their relative tightness/looseness. The other plots their aggressiveness/passivity.

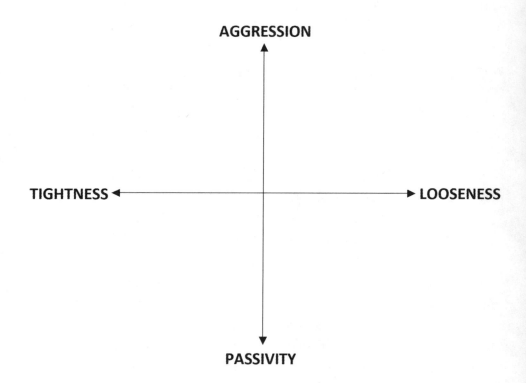

LAGS and TAGS and LAPS and TAPS

If you look closely, every single poker player is his or her own unique type. One could spend an entire lifetime of poker and still be creating different categories to describe players – an exercise that would be so overwhelming as to be impossible. We might even miss the bigger picture as a result. And it's the bigger picture that we need to inform most of our decisions against players at the table. Toward that end, we need to place our opponents into a few – and only a few – categories.

I'm reminded of the plane spotters in England during the Second World War. They were trained by the British government to recognize planes flying over its airspace. But they weren't trained by focusing on the minute detail of each plane. Rather they were given a guidebook that had the basic outline. This general image of the plane was much more effective in helping citizens identify whether the plane was an Allied or an Axis aircraft.

As "poker type" spotters, we need to be aware of the broad outlines of player types, not their finer points. Those finer points may come later. But for our day-to-day, bread-and-butter poker playing, think broad categories.

Specifically, let's focus on four, and then work on a strategy to beat them:

Loose-Aggressive Players (LAGs)

Typically, LAGs are pretty good players who are in a lot of hands. They are dangerous insofar as they will be hard to read since they may be playing a very wide range of hands early on.

Exploiting LAGs

First, try and sit to their left. If possible, you want to see their action before you decide whether and how you will play your hand. This will give you an advantage over them. While it's true that you would have this advantage over any player to your right, it's especially useful when the player is aggressive and in many hands.

Second, narrow the range of hands you play against them. If your range is always at least a little tighter than theirs, you will have a better time of it after the flop.

Third, if you find a LAG's play too distracting – you may be worried about being stacked by guessing wrong or getting caught against the top of their range – consider moving to another table or leaving the game for a while. There is no prize for losing to the best players in the room. You may be better off playing against softer players, or at least players whom you feel more comfortable playing against.

Loose-Passive Players (LAPs)

You may have heard the term "calling station". That's a LAP. In their extreme form they are known as "fish", "guppies", "suckers", and losers. These are ideal opponents. They tend to check and call rather than bet and raise. They play many substandard hands for a call pre-flop, often continuing on the flop, turn, and river – even in the face of aggression. They are often relatively new players who don't know or understand the typically selective starting standards of public poker room players. They are also sometimes just habitual gamblers who like to see how things turn out, and will pay for that privilege.

Exploiting LAPs

Since their calling standards are so low, you should not attempt to bluff a LAP. They will call and you will lose (unless they are calling with a hand so bad that it can't beat your bluff). LAPs are ideal candidates for a value bet, though. They have a hard time folding. On the other hand, their raises are rare, so when they do get aggressive, expect them to have a very strong hand – unless it appears to just be a fatalistic and desperate attempt to bluff or spew a few remaining chips.

Since they are generally bad players, and rarely raise, you are happy to have them on your left. You don't fear raises. You don't fear that they will outplay you once you have committed to a hand.

You will win their money by being aggressive with your strong hands, not by trying to deceive them with slow-plays or bluffs. They will outdraw you sometimes because they play so loosely. But you will make sure that they pay for the privilege, ensuring that when they call they are not getting the right price to do so.

Tight-Aggressive Players (TAGs)

TAGs will play a narrower range than most, and play it aggressively. They will occasionally mix up their play – including some bluff hands in their raising range. And they'll have a few (sometimes very few) marginal hands that they'll raise with in position.

Exploiting TAGs

TAGs are often among your tougher opponents as they tend to play well when they are in a hand. Even so, there are general weaknesses that you can exploit. Some TAGs find it hard to get off their hand, once they initiate the action, since they don't play many of them to begin with. They don't want to fold once they're in – and they can be so focused on extracting maximum value that they miss the signs of strength that their opponents demonstrate. You can sometimes use that trait to your advantage, taking chances on moderately long-shot draws on the flop, knowing that if the draw comes in, you may well stack your sticky opponent. (It's less effective on the turn, since they tend to make drawing expensive.) You must be careful with this strategy, however, as you and your TAG opponent will need to be deep enough to make such a play worthwhile, and you'll need to find a good way to extract the full stack from your solid opponent. That's not always an easy feat.

You can also exploit a TAG by avoiding confrontations with them if you're not very strong – and by playing aggressively against them when you are. The good thing is that TAGs don't play many hands. They are highly selective. They are not as tight as a rock, and are more aggressive, but they are very tight nevertheless. You can avoid them while still playing a good percentage of your strong hands. Depending on how tight they are, you might not mind them on your left. They won't be in that many hands against you, since they're not in that many hands to begin with.

As thinking players, you can sometimes fool them into making mistakes by representing a hand with your betting action. They are good candidates for the well-timed bluff or semi-bluff, and they may be trapped if you show passivity with a very strong hand. Don't overdo the trickery, as they are generally perceptive and have good memories for such actions, and are unlikely to be taken in by it consistently.

Tight-Passive Players, (TAPs):

These are also known as weak-tight or timid players. They play few hands, and they fold them readily to any pressure. They are often just passing time in the poker room, playing for the comps, the companionship, and maybe because they just enjoy being there. They exert little pressure unless they are really loaded, and they can often be backed off their hand if you are aggressive.

How to Exploit TAPs

You're going to increase your percentage of bluffs against TAPs as they'll be more likely to back down. On the other hand, if they resist folding, or come out raising, expect them to be loaded. They're not likely to do this without a very strong hand. If that's the case, just give them no action at all.

Other Player Types

There are other terms used to describe opponents. Here's a list of the most common ones, with an explanation of each, and a brief explanation of how to exploit them.

Fish

This is someone who is really clueless – and who has some money to lose. A fish calls too much, raises too seldom, is easy to read, and doesn't know what he is doing much of the time. He is a sub-category of a LAP. He may have some of the mannerisms of a serious player. He may flick in and stack his chips with great manual dexterity. But he isn't a good player for many reasons – chief among them that he plays sub-standard hands – and plays them for too much money and for too long.

> **Exploiting Fish:** Play your best straightforward game. They barely know their own hand, so don't use deception to trick them.

Maniac

This is someone who is hyper-aggressive and plays a huge range of hands. I'm not talking about a LAG, but a LAG on steroids. A maniac can be playing 100 percent of the cards he receives and may shove with them if his mood dictates it. He may play hands without looking. Maniacs will post voluntary straddles of many multiples of the big blind and may go all-in blind. One word of warning. Some excellent players try to appear as maniacs. But when you really follow their betting action, they are disciplined, even as their mannerisms make themselves appear to be betting without restraint.

> **Exploiting Maniacs:** Stay out of their way unless you have at least a fairly strong hand. Don't try to fool them. If you can, isolate them so you can take advantage of their overly aggressive play. Don't forget that even if they are raising with very little, others in the hand may have you beat.

Rock

(also known as "nit") These are extremely tight players. People with little or no gamble in them. They are extremely careful pre-flop and then rarely bet or raise on or after the flop unless they have a really strong hand. Don't expect a rock to be betting on the come or bluffing. They are in few hands and often play very short stacked – so at most they'll lose the minimum. They can easily be bullied. Within their very tight range they tend to be aggressive. So if a rock actually does raise, don't play against them unless you are loaded.

> **Exploiting Rocks:** There's an expression that applies to this type of player: "Don't feed the nit." It makes sense. No need to try and win money off of them with cleverness. Just avoid them if they're in unless you're loaded.

ABC Player

Someone who is "by the book", who plays very conventionally and does not mix up their play with bluffs or other deception. They are typically TAGs with the flaw of excessive predictability. If they are raising in early position you can count on them to have a premium starting hand. They have no bluffs in their range. If they are calling, they have the pot odds to do so. They can be expected to fold to pressure, unless they have a good reason to call.

> **Exploiting ABC Players:** Make sure to think about what their action means. They are highly unlikely to be acting deceptively, so play against them as if their cards were face up. As is the case with most players, they will tend to see in you the traits that they themselves have adopted. So tend to be aggressive against them, and watch them fold.

Sticky

Someone who may be tight early on – only playing very few starting hands – but who is very reluctant to fold as the action increases. Expect them *not* to fold to a bluff on the turn or river, for example. Similarly, they may push their strong starting hands too long, trying to force them into victory with aggression.

> **How to Exploit Sticky Players:** Don't try to bluff them or confront them with aggression, expecting them to fold. Let them continue to be the aggressor – even if you judge yourself to be far in the lead. When they start with a strong hand they will frequently spew all of their chips as long as you don't give them cause to think you're strong.

Tricky

A tricky player uses a lot of deception. They're often acting strong when they have a weak hand and acting weak when they have a strong hand. They do not play straightforwardly.

How to Exploit Tricky Players: There is no simple answer to this, as tricky players are often, by definition, changing up their game. Even so, recognizing that they may not be representing the true strength of their hand, you may broaden your range by playing more medium strength hands against them. I suggest adopting a style akin to something from table tennis. In table tennis, where players impart great spin on the ball, there is a rubber called "anti-spin". It does not impart spin itself. Rather it tends to neutralize the spin of an opponent, allowing the player to better and more accurately return a ball that has a great deal of spin on it. Similarly, adopt a style of play akin to anti-spin rubber. Do not look to use much trickery or aggression. Play neutrally by tending to check and call rather than bet and raise until and unless you are confident that you are ahead. Until then, let them be the aggressor.

Chapter Eight

Getting Better: Further Improving Your Game

You have learned a very disciplined method of winning money from mediocre and poor players, starting with a very narrow pre-flop range, and playing it aggressively. Now you need to learn some skills that will be necessary to take your game to the next level. Specifically, we'll cover plays like floating, three-betting light, and squeeze plays, as well as how to broaden your range so you can play more hands profitably. We'll also address some of the common pitfalls of good players who are not yet great players – and how to overcome them.

What you'll learn: A selection of additional skills to improve your all-round game further and equip you for even tougher battles.

Why it's important: You can never have too many weapons, and these skills are necessary for you to win even more money from bad and mediocre opponents, while holding your own and beating the better players you're likely to face.

Variance is Your Friend

Many new players fall into the trap of learning one thing too well. They learn how to play tightly and aggressively, thinking that by embracing a narrow range and playing it very strongly they will increase their chances of winning and diminish their variance. If they only play cards superior to their opponents, and play them very aggressively, how can they lose in the long run?

There's something to that. It is important to focus on high value cards, especially when you are starting out. And it's important to play aggressively when you have the goods. But it's also important that you recognize that winning requires risk. There are few if any sure things in poker.

You win in the long run in poker by making good bets – not by only making strong bets on sure things. While at first it helps to focus on those good bets that are close to being sure things, you eventually need to open up a little, and also get your opponents to make bad bets.

The disparity between how good the bet is for you and how bad the bet is for your opponent is the gauge you want to use. This is different from a gauge that embraces bets that are as close as possible to sure things.

Here's an example.

> I have A♠-A♦. My opponent has a draw. The board is K♠-K♦-A♥-A♠. I have seen his cards. He has exactly Q♠-J♠ – a draw to a royal. There is $100 in the pot. We each have $10,000 remaining. I really know his play. He is moderately loose. He will absolutely call up to $500 and see his next card. He will fold for any bet over $500. Do I bet $500 and get him to call, with one out for hitting his royal? Or do I bet $1,000, get him to fold, and win the pot right now?

I hope you picked the $500 bet.

Why is that the better bet? It's the better bet because though there is a tiny chance he'll hit his straight flush by drawing another card (a 45-to-1 shot) and though a bigger bet would guarantee me the pot, the pot odds of 6-to-1 are much smaller than the drawing odds of 44-to-1, making it a terrible bet for my opponent. My $1,000 bet would be forcing him into making the *right* move, when he-would have made the terrible move for $500.

This is an extreme example, but situations come up regularly when you face opponents who are good enough to fold for very large bets, but not good enough to fold for bets that are smaller, even if the pot odds don't favor them.

Here are a few examples.

Exercise 26

Good Bets Versus Bad Bets

Here are some hand scenarios in which you have two choices of what to bet. Pick the correct option. (In all situations imagine a $500 effective stack and an average opponent.)

It's the turn. The pot is $200. You have A♥-K♥. The board is A♦-Q♠ 6♠-6♣. You have two pair with top kicker. By your betting and your opponents calling, you are sure he is on a spade flush draw. You are first to act. How much should you bet?

a) $300.
b) $100.

It's the flop. The pot is $40. You have Q♦-Q♠. The flop is J♦-2♣-2♠. Villain bets $25. You assume his range is J-9+. You raise. How much should you raise?

a) $50.
b) $150.

Answer to Exercise 26

In both of these examples, the larger bet or raise would probably have gotten Villain to fold. But the fold would have been a correct action by him. You don't want to push an opponent into making the correct action, when it would be possible to get him to make the error of calling. While you would reduce your variance with your larger bet, you would be likely to diminish your profit in the long run.

Here are some other "moves" that may increase your variance, but that will help you extract extra money from your opponents.

Floating

The "float play" or "floating" is a very simple countermeasure you can take when your opponent seems to c-bet too much or when you have a particularly tight and straightforward image. You don't want to do it habitually or you'll be noticed – and your opponents will make adjustments. But it is very effective against the aggressive post-flop bettor.

Here's how it works.

You have a hand that is far below your typical three-betting standards. You have position on your overly aggressive opponent. When he bets you call in position, with the intention of taking the hand away from him by being aggressive on a later round. You "float" him – that is you call his bet without the usual strength of hand you require – because you believe that he is being unduly aggressive with a hand that doesn't warrant it. You will then take over the aggression yourself and get him to release his hand.

Here's an example.

You are on the button with A♥-4♥. A bunch of you called the BB when nobody raised. Six of you see the flop. It missed you completely. It's checked to the CO – a player who can't seem to resist trying to steal. He makes it 6BB. You whiffed, but with everyone else having checked, and with this action freak pushing, you figure you might be able to take the hand away from him on a later street. So you call – "floating" his bet. The turn is another nothing card that doesn't connect with your hand. It helps you not at all. Your opponent, true to form, makes a 10BB bet. You make it 25BB, representing that you have a very strong hand. He folds, convinced that you do – or perhaps having nothing himself.

The crowd goes wild while you rake in the pot. A successful float play!

Exercise 27

Floating

1) You have an aggressive opponent who almost always continues to bet on the flop after being aggressive pre-flop. You are on the BTN with J♥-10♥. You called his $10 raise pre-flop. The flop is A♠-9♥-6♠. Villain bets $15. What is a creative play you can sometimes make?

   a) Bluff raise – represent an ace.

   b) Turtle – fold no matter what your drawing odds are.

   c) Float – call with the intention of raising if the turn is a blank.

2) You have a very rocky opponent, who plays a narrow range, and rarely bets or raises without a very strong hand. He makes it $10, three other players call, and you call on the BTN with J♥-10♥. The flop is A♠-9♥-6♠. Villain bets $40. The one other player calls. You should?

a) Raise to $100, representing that you have an ace or better.

b) Fold.

c) Float – Call with the intention of raising a safe turn card.

Answer to Exercise 27

1) c) This is a perfect example of a float play.

2) b) This would be a very bad time for a float as you will have two opponents and a villain who is not someone who regularly c-bets. Wait for a better opportunity.

Three-Betting Light

Here's another wrinkle you can put in your typically well-ironed persona at the table.

You're generally viewed as someone who bets and raises for value – only occasionally throwing in the deceptive play. It can be especially effective in many $1/2 games for you to show three-bet aggression without your standard high value hand. This "move" of a pre-flop raise is said to be "three-betting light" as your hand value is lighter than it might normally be.

Here's an example.

> You are in the CO with a medium strong hand – let's say K-Q. It's below the range of what you would typically need to three-bet in this game (typically J-J+, A-K, A-Qs+). The hand is folded to the LJ seat, occupied by Ernie, a fairly active opponent. He raises to 3BB. The HJ folds. The action comes to you, with K♥-Q♠. Normally you'd fold this hand. It tends to be dominated by pre-flop raising hands like A-K, A-Q, and it is only very slightly ahead of lower pairs that also might be raising. But since you have a very tight and straightforward image you elect to three-bet. Everyone but Ernie folds. He may fold too. Surely he would if he were just trying to win with a naked bluff. He might even fold with a low pair – convinced that you only make the move with what would be a very dominant hand or, at best, a hand of roughly equal value like a big ace.

If your three-bet doesn't win you the pot right there, and there is a flop, you will almost surely fold if he bets. But if he checks, something you expect most of the time, you will bet – and expect to take down the pot.

As with many plays, the risk is that your opponent, loose and wild though he may be, is wise to your act and may take countermeasures. He may four-bet you pre-flop or, more likely, call and then either bet or check-raise the flop. But the advantage is that at this level of no limit, you will only rarely find players sophisticated enough to know what you're doing – and those players will probably be known to you.

Exercise 28

Three-betting light

1) You have 9♥-9♠ on the BTN. Your opponent raises in the HJ seat after the hand is folded to him. The CO folds as well. Typically, though you are

in position, you would fold this hand. But what other line might you consider?

a) Fold. It's a trash hand no matter what the circumstances.

b) Call. And when villain bets the flop, if it's not scary, raise him.

c) Shove. It's a perfect opportunity for a semi-demi-bluff.

d) Raise. This is an example of three-betting light. It will probably cause him to fold. If not he is likely to check the flop and your bet will likely take down the pot.

2) You have a $300 effective stack. You have Q♥-9♥. You are the BB. Four players call and the BTN raises to $20. It is your action.

a) Make it $80. As a tight player this three-bet will likely get everyone to fold.

b) Call. You'll make your surprise bluff by donk-betting the flop.

c) Fold. You are out of position, have many opponents, and your medium strength hand is not worth playing, even if you think the BTN is bluffing.

d) Shove. A perfect time for the semi-demi-bluff.

Answers to Exercise 28

1) d) This is a perfect example of three-betting light. You get extra points deducted for picking c).

2) c) This would not be a good time for three-betting light. Deduct extra points for d.

The Squeeze Play

A squeeze play seeks to take advantage of one player's pre-flop aggression and another's corresponding passivity. It requires you to show strength and apply pressure on both of them. Here's how it typically works.

One player raises. Another calls. And you, the third player in the hand (all others yet to act or having folded), raise. You want at least a hand that has a fairly good chance of improvement – not complete garbage.

The idea is to either steal the hand right there or to steal it on the next card when your remaining opponent checks to you. And you also want some chance of improving to a strong hand.

The thinking behind it is that the initial raise showed some strength – but not necessarily a huge amount. So you wouldn't attempt this play against a very tight player. Surely you wouldn't waste it on a nit (Remember, don't feed the nit!).

The call from the second player showed some degree of weakness. Your raise will convince the first player that you must be very strong as three-bets after a player has called indicate a very strong range. You will also have position on him. So the first player folds even if he has a pretty good hand. Similarly, the second player folds because his hand wasn't that good to begin with, and he assumes that if you're three-betting after a call, you must be very strong.

As is true with other "moves" this is best attempted against non-experts who are not familiar with it, but who are at least good enough to observe what other players are doing. It is best executed when you are seen as relatively tight and straightforward. It's not worth considering if you are seen as a maniac, as your opponents are not likely to respect your action. If you are viewed as a LAG, your opponents are very sophisticated, or if you overuse it, your opponents are likely to take countermeasures – like calling your three-bet and then betting into you, or check raising you on the flop.

Here's an example of a squeeze play.

> You are the CO with A♥-6♥. UTG, UTG+1, UTG+2 fold. UTG+3 raises to $10. All players fold to the HJ who calls $10. Though you wouldn't normally three-bet with this suited ace, it has a decent chance of improving in case the squeeze doesn't work. So you decide to attempt a squeeze play and raise to $40. Both opponents fold.

Here's a simple analysis of what happened.

Unless UTG+3 is playing the top of his range or is otherwise extremely tight and only plays a very narrow and strong range, he is likely to fold as he has to fear that you are playing a premium pair and will have position on him for the next three rounds. The second player will probably follow suit. He too will see your aggression as a very strong play. He called initially, rather than three-betting himself, so it's probable that his hand isn't especially strong. He too might see UTG+3 lay down his hand, and is likely to follow suit. If they both do, your play worked.

What do you do if both players don't fold? Sometimes the choice is easy, as your hand improves. In this specific case, with the possibility of picking up a flush draw, a pair of aces, or two pair, you have about a 30 percent chance of improvement. But even the majority of the time when you don't improve, you will generally continue with your play on the flop. The only exception is if either of your opponents show strength by betting – especially if it is a dry board – making it unlikely that an opponent will be on a draw. In that case, if you didn't improve, you will fold.

Exercise 29

Here are some exercises for you to see whether and how to make this squeeze play.

1) Pick all of the ingredients of what makes for a good opportunity for a squeeze play.

    a) Deep stacked opponents.
    b) Players with relatively wide pre-flop ranges.
    c) Two active opponents, one who has raised, the other called.
    d) Three maniacs who are likely to keep raising.
    e) Two nits.
    f) A hand that is at least marginal, with a chance of improvement.
    g) Early position.
    h) A relatively tight image.

Here are some game situations. Simply decide whether or not these are good opportunities for a squeeze play. Unless noted otherwise, all games are $1/2 no limit, $300 effective stacks, 10-handed.

2) You are on the BTN with K♥-8♣. You are generally a tight aggressive player, but you've had second best hands for the past hour and have been much more active than usual. UTG+1, a nit, raises to $15. All the other players fold to the CO who is a very good TAG. He calls.

3) A LAG in the LJ raises to $10. A poor calling stating in the HJ calls. You have A♠-8♠ in the CO and a very tight image.

4) You are the BB with 10♥-9♥. A loose and rather wild recreational player raises to $10 in the HJ after everyone folds. BTN, an excellent and observant LAG, calls. You are generally very active but have had no cards in an hour, and have folded just about every hand when you weren't the BB.

5) You are the BB with K♦-Q♦. An excellent TAG UTG+2 raises to $15. UTG+3, a rock with a $40 stack, which has gradually diminished from the $200 he started with eight hours ago, calls.

Answers to Exercise 29

1) b, c, f, h. If you put down any other answers re-read this section.

2) Don't squeeze. Just about all of the factors are against you. If a nit is playing a hand for a raise he is probably loaded and will not fold to your raise. The caller may also give you a problem since he is a very good player and may suspect that you are trying to squeeze. Your image is also a problem. Though you are generally tight, the players at the table won't know that since you have acted in a way that makes you appear loose. Also, your hand value is quite low, with little chance of great improvement to the best hand.

3) This is an ideal setup for a squeeze. Your image is tight, your hand has some expectation of improving to a very strong hand if you are called, the initial raiser does so often and may not have much. The caller is a poor player unlikely to suspect you have less than a very strong hand – while he is likely to have called with a middling hand.

4) Though you are not in the ideal late position, this is a good setup for a squeeze. You have a loose player making the initial raise and a perceptive LAG who plays a lot of hands calling what he may suspect is a sub-premium hand. Your raise from the BB may well look to both players like you have a very strong hand – especially given your *recent* image. If your raise doesn't knock them both out, you also have a hand that may hit a strong flop.

5) This is a bad spot for a squeeze. You're out of position. Though we've seen that this in and of itself is not disqualifying, in this situation everything else is pretty much against you. The initial raiser is a tight player, not a loose one, meaning he would be unlikely to raise without a high quality hand from such early position. Similarly, the ultra-tight rock in the UTG+2 calls, meaning a very strong range. And just to make this even less appealing, he is down to his final $25 after he calls. When you raise, he may well just toss in his remaining chips since he's already in for $15. Save your money and fold here.

Changing Gears: Doing the Unexpected

The float play, three-betting light, and the squeeze play are all ways for an otherwise tight-aggressive player to take advantage of his image by playing unconventionally – that is in a manner looser and more aggressive than is typical. There are other situations that arise from time to time when you want to be similarly unpredictable. Every once in a while you want to truly mix up your play – to take advantage of your image in a way that could reward you greatly.

Here are five things to consider when making a very large departure from your typical, disciplined, tight-aggressive style of play. This isn't a formula to be followed, but rather guidelines within which you should operate.

Find Low Cost Opportunities

You should be looking to take advantage of huge implied odds, the kind that sometimes present themselves in a deep-stacked no limit game. For these unexpected actions to bring you a profit in the long run, you need the opportunity to spend very little up front. So, for example, if you are on the button with a nearly worthless hand like low suited connectors, sometimes (not habitually) call the BB or even make a small raise. Do so with an eye on how much you might be able to win. But only do so when the money to enter the hand is relatively small and the amount you might win, as reflected in the stack size of your opponents, is great.

Do so When the Reward is Enormous

You're looking to stack someone worth stacking, or win a big chunk from a huge stack. If someone with a short stack shoves, you're not looking to isolate him with some unconventional play. But if you can get in cheaply against a deep stack, that might entice you to play.

Rely on a Well-established Image

Unconventional plays work best when, for whatever reason, you are seen by your opponents as being particularly one way or another. If you've been in a lot of hands, showed down some clear bluffs, and seem to have everyone thinking you're a wild man, then you might want to play a really big hand particularly aggressively – even if your standard play would be to be really slow with it. More typically, you will be viewed as a tight player. That will come from the relatively narrow range of hands you play, especially in early and middle position. Accordingly, most of your unconventional plays will take advantage of your tight image. One word of warning: Make sure you understand what your image really is, not just what you think of yourself.

Think Through the Whole Play From Beginning to End

You need to plan the entire sequence of actions you'll take in a hand and ensure they follow a logical arc. Just thinking, "I've been tight, I'll raise" is an error. Instead, consider the whole hand – and how you would play pre-flop, flop, turn and river. If you're going for a squeeze play, think about what you'll do if you're called by one player. If a player bets into you on the flop or turn, don't stubbornly stick to your plan to bet them out of the pot. Recognize that the correct line to follow is to fold.

Pay Attention to the Reaction to your Unconventional Play
Along the lines of the last consideration, you've got to be willing to suspend your plan if you see a reaction that isn't as you planned. Players sometimes fall victim to their own cleverness by continuing with a play even when it's clear that it's not selling. An example of this is three-betting pre-flop and being faced with a donk-bet on the flop. Yes, maybe your opponent is only testing you. And maybe a raise would get him to fold. But at this level it's much more likely that in spite of only calling your pre-flop three-bet, your opponent just hit a great flop and now judges himself to be ahead of you. Either that, or your three-bet didn't convince him you were strong, and he's now trying to re-steal by showing unconventional out-of-position aggression. Either way, your plan failed – and if you didn't improve, you need to get away from the hand and fold.

Exercise 30
1) Pick from the list below all of the examples of reasons you might want to mix up your game?
    a) You are fairly sure you have a well-established image as a tight player.
    b) Your opponents are really, really bad.
    c) Almost all of your opponents are observant.
    d) There are a few very deep stacks in play.
    e) You have been very inactive lately.
    f) You have been hit by the deck and are on a colossal winning streak.
    g) The dealer has been flashing cards unintentionally.
    h) The player to your right is extremely loose.
    i) You have a great read on some of the better players.

2) If you have made an attempt at a squeeze play, and the initial raiser calls your three-bet, and the caller folds, what should you tend to do, if you haven't improved, if the pot is checked to you on the flop?

    a) check behind.

    b) bet.

3) Which statement is not a serious consideration when deciding to mix up your play?

    a) Winners never quit and quitters never win.

    b) If your attempt to win doesn't happen as planned, and your opponent shows unexpected strength, generally fold.

    c) Think through your entire line from the beginning.

    d) When considering your attempt to change gears, look for big potential gain and low risk.

4) Who is your target audience when you mix up your play?

    a) Your true expert.

    b) A solid, observant, good player.

    c) A compulsive gambler who can't resist a good game.

    d) A terrible player.

Answers to Exercise 30

    1) Relevant are a, c and e. You want a well-established image before you think about mixing up your play. That means that you have to have opponents who are good enough to at least consider what type of player you are. The other considerations are interesting but not germane to whether you change gears.

    2) b) bet. Most of the time, if your opponent has checked to you, it indicates weakness, and your bet on the flop will get him to fold.

    3) a) This is a terrible aphorism when applied to poker.

    4) b) They have to be good enough and observant enough to notice what you're doing.

Chapter Nine

Get Your Mind Right to Play Winning Poker

In this chapter we will address the "meta-game" in poker – an area that is crucial for helping the good player become and stay a winning player. Broadly, this encompasses all the issues related to the game that do not specifically involve cards and chips. For instance, we'll look at the subject of keeping records, so you can really see and understand how you are doing. We'll delve into tells – and how they can be both useful and potentially misleading. And we'll look at the stack-crushing arena of steaming – also known as tilt – what it is, how it works, and how to avoid it.

What you'll learn: How to develop the discipline and powers of observation necessary to always play your best game.

Why it's important: All the skills in the world won't help you if you don't have your mind right to play winning poker.

Introduction

I love old movies. One of my favorites is *Cool Hand Luke*. It's about a character, Luke, played by Paul Newman, who is jailed for an act of public vandalism, and sentenced to a prison chain-gang. It's an awful prison, with a sadist for a prison boss. Early in the movie, this boss is addressing the new prisoners, including Luke. He tells them that if they are to get along in this prison they must get their mind right. Newman runs afoul of the rules, never does get his mind right, and suffers the serious consequences.

Every time I watch it I think of poker. The same aphorism applies. If you want to succeed at the poker table you must get your mind right. There are many players who have the technical skills to be winners, but who lose nevertheless. There are reasons for this. In this chapter we'll explore some of the losing habits of otherwise good players — and address each in turn. The first is about being honest with ourselves — by keeping clear, simple, and regular records of our play.

Keeping Records

We are often our own worst enemies at the poker table. We aren't honest with ourselves about our results. We often fall victim to the Dunning-Kruger effect. This is a cognitive bias in which people mistakenly think they are better than they are. It is the technical term for something that the American Automobile Association observed when they asked people to rate themselves as drivers. Over 90 percent reported themselves to be "better than average". Statistically, that's impossible of course. But drivers are well known for having an inflated sense of their own skill.

Poker players are also notorious for suffering from this. Ask casual players how they do at poker, and you'll typically hear them tell you that they "just about break even" or are "maybe a little ahead". They take their optimistic view of their own talents to another level — a more dangerous one — by seeing even their measurable ends through the distorted lens of their own misperception.

There may be no antidote for the Dunning-Kruger effect among drivers. It's difficult to know how you could objectively determine your own driving skills. Not so for poker. You can easily get a simple, easily understood, and accurate picture of your own abilities. Simply keep good records!

You will need a measuring stick, with which you can plot your progress or, if necessary, your regress as a poker player. Toward that end, you need to record your sessions so you can see where you stand, what the trends are, and where the leaks are. You won't see everything about your play by keeping records. But you'll do a much better job of self-analysis than if you try to do so without records.

Keeping records is simple – though not necessarily easy. There are apps you can get for your phone or other mobile device. Use one. Or do it by hand in a small notebook as I do. It's the substance of the data you record that's most important more than the vehicle you use.

Here's an exercise for you. Set up a record keeping system that will track how you do. Record the following information for every poker session:

- ♠ Date you played.

- ♠ Where you played (if online, what site).

- ♠ What game you played, at what stakes.

- ♠ How much you won or lost.

- ♠ A running tally of how much you are up or down.

- ♠ When your session began and when it ended.

- ♠ Total duration of your session.

- ♠ A running tally of how much you have played for the year.

- ♠ Notes about the session, your play, and the players you faced.

It's likely to look something like this:

Date	Location	Game	Win/loss YTD	Hours	Notes
1/16	c: A'star	$2/5 nlhe	+$628 +$3,452	7p-3a 8/86	Joey B. on tilt.
1/18	h:BVG	$10-20 lt	+$451 +$3,903	9p-1a 4/90	Love limit.
1/23	c:A'star	$2/5 nlhe	+$1,178 +$5,081	8p-3a 7/97	Won coin flips.
1/25	h:Arnie	PL dc $2ante	-$511 +$4,581	6p-4a 10/107	Harry on my left.

I also make a special note when a session is in a home game and when it is in a casino (using an "h" or "c" respectively) to make it easier for me to divide out the results for purposes of analysis. Similarly, though I include all of my tournament results in with my cash game results, I make a note that allows me to easily separate the two. I want to be able to see how I am doing in cash games, tournaments, and overall.

Now fill in the information for your most recent session. Take your time. Make sure you've got it right. Commit yourself to doing this after each poker session. If you can do this actually at the poker table, all the better. You want to write down the specifics immediately. You can transfer it to your permanent database later at home. Believe me when I tell you that if you don't keep track of this immediately – right when you are done with your session – you will forget some of this information by the time you are home. And you might forget to record the session entirely.

If you are already doing this, great. But make sure that you are including all of the information I have suggested above. You have to keep track of every session or it won't work. Just to put a fine point on it, you can't discount a session because you took a terrible bad beat or because you otherwise considered the session an outlier. You can't fail to include the big tournament entry fee at the World Series of Poker just because you want your numbers to look good. Realize that this is just for you (and the IRS too, I suppose, if you are planning on paying taxes on your winnings). So be honest!

Once you get in the habit of entering this information, you need to use it to analyze how you are doing.

Your first and most important piece of data is your total win/loss number. Is it in the red or the black? Are you up or down? If it's up you are making a profit at the game. If it's down you're losing. There may be many explanations for it. There may be many stories – anecdotes of bad beats, suck outs, misplayed hands by your opponents, injections of tremendous amounts of good luck or bad luck. But, bottom line, are you a winning player or a losing player? These records will inform you accurately.

But it's not the entire story, not by a long shot. You also need to be able to drill down deeper to understand some of the why behind the what. How long are your winning and losing sessions? Maybe you do better when you devote many hours to a playing session. Maybe the reverse is true. What time of day is the most profitable? Similarly, perhaps certain casinos or online sites may prove more or less profitable than others. You may not be able to immediately understand why, but just knowing that it is so is a useful fact.

You must not be too quick to draw conclusions about the data you review. If you are a part-time player, your sample size may be insufficient for you to learn anything significant at first about the real playing conditions on a site or in a poker room. The fact that you lost on three separate occasions, with sessions lasting two or three hours, may tell you absolutely nothing about the quality of the games there. You might have just had an understandable string of bad luck. The games might typically be great. On the other hand, if you never seem to win in the $2/5 game at the Bellagio, in spite of having visited there for 300 hours this past year, then it might not be for you. You might find that you crushed the $2/5 game at the Aria during a similar 300 hour stretch, suggesting you might just play better at the Aria, or the typical lineup may be more profitable for you. Maybe the game there is softer, or maybe there is a regular at the Bellagio who just has your number. Or maybe all of your Bellagio sessions took place right after you busted out of their daily tournament – while your Aria sessions always take place late at night, when you stop there after your job. Again, the key is keeping accurate and detailed records so you can review and analyze them later.

Different online sites have different qualities to them as well. You might figure out what it is about a particular room that makes it the most profitable place. But even if you don't, it's useful to know that of the 30 sessions you had at one place, 20 of them were unprofitable. While the 30 sessions you had at another place, all of them were profitable. You might not figure out exactly why. But even if you don't, it would be worth knowing. You might stop playing some place just because your results are consistently worse than playing some place else – even if you can't figure out why that is so.

Similarly, you want to see clearly and simply what game you played and what your win/loss was for every session. You'll want to know, for example, if you are winning money at $1/2, but only breaking even at $2/5 – and getting crushed in $1/3 PLO. You'll want to also have a record of your tournament play – with the size of the tournament, the entry fee, the location of the tournament, and how you did. This may help you focus your attention on improving a particular game, or deciding to avoid it in the future, while focusing your efforts in more profitable waters.

I also suggest you leave some space in your records for general notes about the playing session. These may be as brief as "Couldn't stay awake" to details about some of the players you encountered, or things you noticed about yourself, or even some sketched out hand histories. Of course, if you're playing online, or have software of some kind that keeps track of all of your hand histories, you can get detailed analysis of how often you voluntarily entered the pot, raised pre-flop, c-bet, etc. That information is extremely useful – as is a similarly detailed picture of your opponents. But again, it is no substitute for your own record keeping.

The key is this: You need records to see how you're doing. That is the first step toward doing better.

One Final Note

Generally accepted poker wisdom is that it takes about 500 hours of play for you to really see if you are beating the game. If you are thoughtful, disciplined, and apply what you are learning and have learned at poker, you may reach a point in your poker career when you have played 500 hours and are in the black. Generally speaking, this will mean that you are good enough to consistently beat the other players in the game and the rake or time charge. It may be by a small amount. It may happen in the first 500 hours you play, or it may take you a few years to achieve. But sooner or later, if you apply what you've learned and are diligent, this may well happen.

When this happens – when you have a consistent record of winning that lasts for at least 500 or so hours of play – I want you to stop playing, at least for a day. Pause. And then celebrate. Don't go crazy. But celebrate your achievement. You have just done something that fewer than 10 percent of all poker players do. You have ceased to be a losing player. Congratulations. You are now part of the non-losing few.

Exercise 31

This one is really easy and simple. But it may take you 30 minutes nevertheless.

Buy a notebook – a wide ruled one. Open it to the second page, so you are looking at two pages at one time. Divide the first page into eight roughly equal columns as identified above. The second page is space for notes from the session. If you need more than one line continue on the line below it.

Record your last four sessions – or as many as you can remember. Try hard to get each of the entries as accurate as possible. It may take some time. That's okay.

Now go to the App store on your phone. Find an app that allows you to record all of this information on your device for easy reference and computations. Make sure you have one that works for you. Plan on taking your notebook and physically writing in it the next time you play. Bring it with you to the table. It will serve as an immediate reminder that before you leave the poker room you need to record exactly how you did, how long you played, etc. If you find the right app, transfer the information to it – and then record directly to it after every session. Use your notebook to keep notes about your play, questions, and thoughts for you to ponder in between sessions.

Common Mistakes of Otherwise Good Players

You might have a lot of poker skill. You might understand pot odds, drawing odds, implied odds, fold equity, Game Theory Optimization, and you might be good at deception, and how to stay out of the way of strong, aggressive players. But you're still losing and you can't figure out why. Below, I've listed some common mistakes that good players make in spite of their poker skills. Avoid them, and watch your win rate improve.

Poor Game Selection

Many otherwise good players are hurt by their ego. They just can't stand the idea of dropping down in stakes, or moving tables, thinking that it betrays a weakness that others will see. That's wrongheaded thinking for the winning player. What matters is your bottom line, not your reputation. Think about whom you're most likely to win money from, not whom you'd like to be associated with. Play against the losers.

I'm reminded of the great poker player (and super nice guy) Eric Drache. The stories about him are legend. It was said that he was often broke because, though he was the eighth best player in the world, he always played with the seven who were better than him.

There's no award for being beaten by the best players in the room. Seek the softest game with the most potential profit. That may not be the biggest game you can afford either. Though your status may increase the bigger your play, you might actually find that you can grind out more money per hour at $1/2 than at $2/5.

Some players are loath to move their table or their seat once they sit down. This too is a major problem for otherwise good players. Part of being good is finding the best seat in the best game and being willing to move to it. So get off your duff from time to time to look around the room. See what else is going on. If your game has a bunch of short stacks and nitty players, see if there might be greener pastures elsewhere. And then don't be shy. Feel free to give the floor your name and ask for a table change. Opt for the open seat to the left of the big loose stack. Remember that part of a winner's strategy is being able and willing to find the most profitable place to play.

Not Paying Attention to Opponents

One of the big advantages of playing live as opposed to online is that you get to check out your opponents. Yet many players who generally know what they're doing at the table fail to fully take advantage of the game by not focusing enough on the players they're against. They become habitual and automatic in their play. When you're starting out, developing a certain standardized set of hands that you'll play pre-flop makes sense. It helps you break bad habits of looseness or inattention to position. But you must also pay attention to the type of player you are against. Don't be a first level thinker, only focused on your hand, and playing your cards alone. If you do so you will miss many opportunities for profitable action.

Here's one obvious behavior to look out for. Many players, including fairly good ones, anticipate the betting action and broadcast in advance that they are going to fold. If they are acting behind you, and you notice this, you can take advantage of it by stealing them blind. While it's true that some players cutely try to reverse this on you, few do. When you see an opponent who has yet to act position his cards for a fold, he is almost always about to fold. Other times, players stare at the flop for a second or two longer than normal when they haven't hit, trying desperately to see if they have something worth playing. You will not see either of those obvious tells if you aren't paying attention. So pay attention or fail to reap the rewards. (See the section on tells below.)

Pre-flop Passivity

It's almost surely incorrect to make a practice of only folding or raising pre-flop. But it's not far from correct. Although there are some situations when the good player should call prep-flop, especially in a very loose and passive game, many otherwise good players do this far too often. They let in opponents with poor hands they wouldn't play for a raise. When the flop hits they don't know where they are, and whether the flop helped their opponent. They end up playing far too many hands, and often staying around far too long in the hand, unsure of whether or not they're ahead. Avoid these situations by being decisive pre-flop. That means increasing both your aggressiveness and tightness as the situation demands.

It's true that highly skilled players can profitably play a broad range pre-flop, especially from late position, when most of the other players in the game call. True, you must consider the implied odds you get in a very passive game, allowing you to play more hands pre-flop. All true. But even so, for the most part, many players are costing themselves a lot of money by routinely throwing in the $2 or $3 just because they see a lot of other people doing so. They'd be much better off, most of the time, if they narrowed their range from just about every two card combination, and then raised to 3BB or so – and grabbed positional advantage on future streets.

Feeding the Nit

This is really a subset of the point about paying attention to your opponents above. If you're observant, you'll notice that there are players who play an extremely narrow and strong range pre-flop, and only bet or raise with the nuts or a draw to the nuts. You will spot them if you are even moderately attentive. Just about every room has at least a few. Even so, many players seem to be on a mission to beat these nits. They will call the nits' raises or re-raises and hope to get lucky enough to crush them with a monster.

This is not the way to deal with a very tight player. The simple rule is to not feed the nit. Repeat that. Don't feed the nit. Give him no action whatsoever. Let him have the pot when he bets. Let him bluff you out of the occasional pot. You will be saving your money in the long run. Repeat after me: "Don't feed the nit!"

Not Respecting Large Bets

Players in $1/2 and $1/3 games do bluff. Don't get me wrong. They include bluffs in their pre-flop raising range; they frequently make c-bets with nothing; and they even sometimes bluff the turn and the river. Fair enough. But most of the time – the vast majority of the time in fact – when they make a large bet they have a strong hand.

Good players, sometimes even very strong players, get into trouble by over-thinking situations and discounting the likelihood that their opponent has the hand he is representing. Perhaps this survives from limit poker, when the limit bet on the turn or the river was only a small fraction of the pot. We were taught in those games that folding a winner on the river was a huge mistake, while calling the limit bet incorrectly was a small mistake.

But in no limit hold'em, when the bet on the turn and the river can be as large or even larger than the pot itself, this is surely a mistake. If someone bets half the pot on the river, you have to be at least fairly sure he's bluffing (33 percent sure to be precise) for your call to make sense. From my experience, bluffs aren't being made at nearly that frequency. Most of the time, the vast majority of the time, when your opponent makes a significant bet, he has a very strong hand. Judge the situation on a case-by-case basis of course. But typically your fold will save you a lot of money.

Exercise 32

We've covered this material elsewhere in this book. So regard these questions as a review.

1) Which of the following characteristics would you look for in a game?
   a) Tough players who could challenge me – like in tennis.
   b) Players with short stacks whom I could dominate with my big stack.
   c) Weak, feeble players – the more fish the better.
   d) Solid, observant, generally predictable tight-aggressive players.

2) What should you do if you don't think the game you are in is profitable?
   a) Look around for a better game, and see the floor about moving to it.
   b) Tighten up, narrow your range, and protect your stack.
   c) Try and get your opponents to go on tilt by acting rudely.
   d) Adopt a wild and aggressive style to loosen up the game.

3) You are in a very loose and passive game. Which answer describes when you would best play 10♠-5♠?
   a) In late position only, and only for a call, and only if there were no raise.
   b) In late position only, but only for a raise, and only if it were folded to you.
   c) Never, under any circumstances.
   d) For a check, if you were the large blind and the pot was not raised.

4) You have A♦-7♣ in middle position. The pot has been raised to $12 by a LAG under the gun. Another player has called. The action comes to you. You should?
   a) Fold.
   b) Raise to $24.
   c) Call.
   d) Raise to $36.

5) You are on the BTN with K♠-K♥. Three players called the $2 BB. You raised to $16. You got two callers. The flop was A♠-J♥-8♦. The first player bets $35. The second player folds. You should?
   a) Fold.
   b) Call.
   c) Raise to $70.
   d) Raise to $105.

6) You are in early position in a $1/3 no limit game. There's a $300 maximum buy-in. Though you now have a stack of $400, you have had to re-load several times and have lost $600 over the five hours you've been playing. One suckout after another. You're dealt Q♥-Q♦ in UTG+1. It's folded to you. You should?
   a) fold.
   b) call.
   c) raise to $10.
   d) raise to $6.

7) You're in the CO and raised to $10 with A♥-Q♥ following a pre-flop call from an early position nit. He unexpectedly called your raise. You have an effective stack of $300. The flop is K♦-J♦-4♥. Villain checks. You bet $15. Villain raises you to $50. What do you do?
   a) Call – you have seven outs to make a pair of aces or an inside straight – all of which would be better than his likely pair of kings. There's also a backdoor flush possibility. If you hit you'd surely get his stack.
   b) Fold – don't feed the nit.
   c) Raise to $150 – he's probably semi-bluffing with a flush draw. Give him a bad price for his draw.
   d) Shove – he's probably bluffing and this would surely get him to fold.

Answers to Exercise 32

1) c) If you got this wrong please re-read this section and go back to Chapter 1.

2) a) While the other answers might be useful if you were unable to move, the best answer is certainly a).

3) d) This is a trash hand and should be folded, unless you have no choice in the matter. Partial credit for c – as you got the right idea.

4) Fold. There's no reason to call, and surely no reason to raise.

5) Fold. His bet means something. If he were weak he could have checked and hoped to get a free card with you checking. Respect the significant bet. He almost surely hit the ace or better (even though he may be bluffing).

6) c) Don't change your play just because you've been losing and are dispirited. If you've really lost your taste for poker for the day you should leave. But as long as you're in the hand, play with the appropriate aggression.

7) b) Don't feed the nit. His range includes a king, but it also includes Q-Q and K-K (and maybe also 4-4). You must be observant and responsive to your opponents. And remember, "don't feed the nit"

Tells

A "tell" is an unintentional physical action, movement, or behavior of some sort that tends to give away the true strength of an opponent's hand. The action "tells" you what the strength of the opponent's hand is, even though the player would prefer it not do so.

Poker fiction, especially as it appears in the movies, loves to focus on these tells. A player fiddles with his ring when he's bluffing; a player moves his hand through his hair when he has a good hand; the otherwise tough opponent has an eye that bleeds when he's nervous; the expert player is so cool and collected that he exhibits no tells. In fact, if you were to ask a non-player to name the one thing he knows about winning at poker he might very well say, "Keep a poker face". There's even a Lady Gaga song with that title, *Poker Face*.

But that's showbiz. In reality, most players, especially new or otherwise non-winning players, think too much about tells.

There are wonderful books on the subject. Mike Caro has one, Zach Elwood and Joe Navarro each have a couple. You can dig a little to find others. But let me caution you. Generally speaking, tells are overrated. Just ask any online pro, who must succeed with no physical tells whatsoever. You usually don't need to be able to read tells to gain an edge over a mediocre or poor opponent.

Many tells, identified carefully and well by these and other authors, fall into a category of actions people unconsciously take that betray nervousness. We tend to cross our legs when we're uncomfortable, cover our mouths, rub our faces, or do whatever when we are feeling under stress. Fair enough. The problem, however, is that most of the time, we don't know whether our opponent is showing anxiety because he is weak or whether he is anxious about how strong his hand is. It could also be that he has restless leg syndrome, or is generally uptight when he plays. He might have a bad case of gas. We might notice the action but not really have much of a handle on whether it means strength or weakness or nothing at all to do with poker.

There are usually more reliable indicators as to an opponent's strength. Most of the time, players betray the true strength of their hand by their very conscious and obvious betting action. Focus on that, and the nature of the player, and their perception of you and your type of play, and you will have nearly all of the pieces of the puzzle that you'll need to be a winning player.

Even so, while focusing on tells often works to distract you from the more important work at hand of responding to the conscious betting action, there are some simple tells that are worth learning. I call these "giveaway tells".

Giveaway Tells

These are actions taken by generally unsophisticated players that can help you evaluate the true strength of their hand. (Realize that many players have read the same literature, and watch the same instructional sites, so they may know these too – and reverse them on you.)

Staring at the Flop

This is a common tell of weakness. A player stares at the flop for an extra second or two, trying to find something worthwhile. This demonstrates weakness. Had he hit the flop, he would not continue to stare.

Double-checking Hole Cards

Why does someone check his hole cards? Usually to see what he has (sounds like a chicken crossing the road joke). But why would he need to check if he has two suited cards? This often happens on the turn, when an opponent isn't certain if he has one suited card to match the three on board. When he has two, he normally remembers that when the board has two of that suit on the flop. So when the third hits on the river, he knows he has the flush. Yes, he may be double-checking to throw you off. So you have to be at least a little concerned that it's a false tell. But much of the time – I'd say a substantial majority of the time – it's still reliable. He's on a flush *draw*. Bet into him without being very concerned that he hit the flush.

Looking Down and Then Looking Away

This is usually a sign of strength. The opponent is doing two things. He's checking his chip stack unconsciously because he intends to bet. And then he's looking away to feign indifference. Few players have mastered this well enough to fake it. But it happens very quickly. So you need to be watching as soon as the flop hits to spot it.

Talking About the Hand

I've found this to be one of the most reliable tells when I have a tough decision to make. I check and my opponent shoves. He has a very polarized range. Either he has a monster or he is making a monster bluff. It's very expensive to call. But if I am right about it being a bluff I will make a lot of money. What to do?

If I start to hear him talk I am usually persuaded that he has it. This is because, from my experience, a bluffer doesn't want to attract attention to himself, he just wants the experience to be over. He takes his anxiety and freezes with it, afraid that if he does anything you will catch on that he's bluffing and call him. Someone with a monster hand is usually confident, exuding energy, and eager to release it. Being confident he doesn't mind releasing it with talk. And so he babbles. Not always, but often.

Chip Grabbing

This is fairly good indicator of weakness. A player grabs chips in position hoping to freeze your action by intimidating you with the chips you'll think he is about to bet. More often than not he will check when the action gets to him. I usually bet into someone doing this – even with no hand. He will typically fold. Again, not always, but most of the time.

Betting When Leaving (or Otherwise Pre-occupied)

Players regularly come and go. They talk to their friends. They rake in chips after a big hand. While they will continue to get dealt a hand of poker, they are doing something other than focusing on the game. When this is the case, you can sometimes infer useful information about the true strength of their hand.

In general, a distracted player will tend to fold to any aggression. He doesn't want to be bothered while he is stacking up his chips, getting ready to eat, getting ready to leave for the day, or talking to his friend. He won't tell the dealer to deal him out, since he already posted a blind and is entitled to a free hand. If you're in the CO and a distracted player is on the button, your bet will generally get a fold. But if you see a player engaged in one of the activities above, and yet he bets, tend to believe that the betting action indicates real strength. If you have a mediocre hand or worse, fold.

Other Barriers to Poker Profitability

Much of this book is dedicated to making you a better player, teaching you the skills to make better bets, win more money when you win, lose less when you lose, and improving the percentage of the time that you do win. A lot is focused on learning proper odds – pot odds, drawing odds, and implied odds, while also learning to exploit your opponent's errors in judgment, self-control, or both.

Ideally, you will learn all of these skills and become an overall winning poker player. That's the goal. But there are impediments to achieving that goal that don't involve strategic thinking or action at the table, but rather that involve mental errors and lapses in judgment – even when you know what is correct. I call those unforced errors.

Unforced errors fall into two categories. There are leaks – things that you do that drain your profit, causing your bottom line to suffer as a result. And there is "steaming" when your emotions overtake your thoughtful action.

Leaks

Anything that drains your hard-earned poker money is considered a leak. Gambling at games that favor the house is the typical and probably most common instance of a leak. Players who take poker profits and use them to shoot craps are said to have a leak in their game. Similarly, some winning poker players can't avoid sports betting, or horses, or keno, or even roulette, bingo, or slot machines. It's like having a big pot with a hole in the bottom. No matter how much water you put in it, it will eventually go dry because of the hole. So too with poker profits. If you put them into something that is inherently unprofitable, like craps, roulette, or baccarat, you will eventually drain yourself dry no matter how much you win at poker.

Some players can't avoid leaks like this. To them I recommend that you not play in a public poker room. True, you may well find other outlets for your gambling interests. (Who doesn't know a bookie?) Even so, the temptation to throw away your money at some other table game is best avoided.

Steaming or Going on Tilt

Steaming, also known as "going on tilt" is oft defined as losing control of your game by allowing emotions to carry you away into irrational betting behavior. Excessive steaming has torpedoed many players' bankrolls – and often ruined budding poker careers.

It's important that you recognize your own steam triggers.

Different people have different triggers. Some people absolutely cannot handle being beaten. They can accept a loss. Maybe even two or three in a row. But if they're beaten on for 30 minutes, they just can't play rationally after that. They start to play maniacally and desperately until they lose everything they have on them – and maybe even more than that.

Similarly, some players can't handle winning. Sure, they love winning pots. But once they are significantly ahead of the game – say up a couple of buy-ins – they just can't keep their discipline. They start playing extremely loosely and frivolously, calling and raising with reckless abandon. Before long, their stack is largely depleted.

Others are fine unless they're being drawn out on. They bet when they are ahead, and their game is pretty strong – even if they don't take full advantage of their image by bluffing more. But if someone calls them and then out-draws them to win on the river with a four-outer, they lose it.

Here's a list of some other common triggers. Do any of these send you on tilt?

- ♠ Slow players.
- ♠ Being slow-rolled.
- ♠ Talkative players.
- ♠ Arrogant players.
- ♠ Someone you just can't stand.
- ♠ Folding a hand that would have won.
- ♠ Alcohol.
- ♠ Getting into an argument.
- ♠ Being embarrassed at the table.
- ♠ Being short stacked.
- ♠ Having a huge stack.
- ♠ Being tired.

♠ Having someone watch you play.

♠ Being sleep-deprived.

♠ Playing for a really long time.

You can surely add to the list based on your own experience. Anything that tends to prevent you from playing your best game, or that sets you off into playing emotionally and not rationally, is a tilt trigger.

How to Avoid Tilt

I've found that a few things work in controlling my tilt triggers.

Separate Yourself from the Stimulus

Get into the habit of leaving the table when you start to experience any of these things. Literally get up and walk away. Give yourself 10 or 15 minutes to think about what has happened and what you want your response to be. This break in the action will probably get you to start thinking and stop reacting. But if it doesn't, the cure is easy. Just stay away. Rack up your chips and leave the poker room. There will always be another game.

After a while, you'll need less and less time away from the table to regain your composure and play your best game – until, ideally, you'll be able to shrug off the habitual and emotional response to the stimulus before the next hand gets dealt. But until that time, it's often best to just walk away.

The key is to recognize when you are set off or at risk of being set off, and to have the strength of mind to walk away until you regain your balance.

Adopt a Habit of Taking a Five-minute Break Every Hour or Two

The problem with taking a break from the action only when you experience a tilt trigger is that sometimes, especially when you are relatively new to poker, you don't notice the steaming until it has completely enveloped you and destroyed your ability to walk away. Sometimes you get so angry and bothered by a bad beat or an annoying opponent that your emotions overwhelm the judgment that would have you leave the table. Accordingly, to prevent that from happening for too long, adopt a habit of leaving the table at regular intervals, tilt or no. By the time you have walked away, you will typically be clear-headed enough to recognize that you are steaming, even if you don't have the ability to yet make good poker decisions. Your clarity of thought, limited to knowing that you shouldn't be playing, will sufficiently keep you away until your ability to make rational decisions returns.

Think About your Long-term Results

Admittedly, this doesn't work very well if you're a losing player. But for me, keeping records and knowing that I'm a winning player in the long-run helps calm me down when a particular incident might tend to set me off. Any time I'm upset about a particular hand or even a long losing streak, I just check my records to reinvigorate my ego and reinstall my poker equilibrium.

Chapter Ten

Wrapping it all Up

In this final chapter we'll explore how to put all of these pieces together to get the most out of your poker game – including lifestyle questions, whether and how to turn pro, and how to deal with the psychologically crushing effects of losing streaks.

What you'll learn: An integrated strategy that will prepare you to enter or re-enter the poker world with confidence.

Why it's important: The whole is greater than the sum of its parts.

Continued Learning

One book does not a great poker player make. Surely that's true. If you want to beat the game, including the rake, you'll need to continue to learn.

Poker thinking has evolved over the years. And it will continue to evolve. If you don't keep up with it, you can be assured that others at your table will – and will take advantage of your stunted poker education.

There are many learning opportunities. There are instructional videos online, websites, articles, books, even radio shows and podcasts. All will provide you with something to consider.. I encourage you to do your own digging to find out what other people have found useful.

I have one other suggestion. I've had occasion, as the host of the poker radio show *House of Cards*, to interview many professional poker players. We've chatted about their careers, their accomplishments, and the roots of their poker success. With few if any exceptions, each pro said that their game improved most significantly because of regular poker discussions with other serious poker players. More than any of the other means of acquiring knowledge, poker hand and situation analysis was the most useful.

Finding or building such a discussion group may not be easy for those who aren't already in a poker-player rich environment. What do you do if you don't have a circle of buddies who are serious about their poker? Fortunately, there are some ways to engage in this discussion even if you don't have any serious poker players in your midst.

There are online forums that can serve as a virtual circle. These are sites like Two Plus Two, Cards Chat, and Pocket Fives, among others. You can post questions or thoughts about a poker situation, and solicit responses from people in a vast network. It's a great way to engage in useful and skill-strengthening poker discussion.

Dealing with Losses

Even the very best poker education will not guarantee you consistent success at the table. The greatest players on earth have all suffered soul crushing defeats from time to time. It is part of the territory of regular poker play. Aside from cheating, there is no way to avoid long losing streaks. It just happens.

You need to be prepared for this so that the devastating emotional blow does not completely destroy you. Here are a few suggestions for dealing with these losses that should enable you to ride them out with the bulk of your bankroll and sanity still intact.

Keep Good Records

Lack of knowledge can amplify the significance of a major losing streak by not having a counterbalancing record of your wins. The losing streak will be the most recent event – and as such the most vivid poker image in your brain. Without some objective evidence to the contrary, it may appear that you are doomed to lose, shaking your confidence and your ability to play your best game. Similarly, by keeping an objective record of your play over a long period of time, you will be providing a simple and useful perspective. It should at least soften the psychological impact of the most recent downswing.

Look Closely at Your Game

You want to review your play from time to time. A long series of losing sessions provides an excellent excuse for such analysis. Step back from the table for a while to think through how you have played your hands. Look at very specific situations you were in and the decisions you made. This is often not possible while you are in the heat of a hand. But look at your strategy out of the intense heat of the moment. Would you do again what you did in that situation?

Discuss Critical Hands with Others

As mentioned earlier, it helps to have the benefit of a few people looking at your actions. Dissect some hands. What is the "group think" about your play? Can you detect any pattern in how you've been playing critical hands? Perhaps you've grown too cautious? Aggressive? Passive? Again, it's sometimes tough for us to assess our own actions. So put it out to others to discuss. Make sure you're not defensive. You want others to find errors. It's the only way you're going to improve.

Consider Dropping Down in Stakes

Maybe the game you're in is too tough. It happens. Maybe you are a victim of your early success – moving up to bigger stakes with better players before you're ready. This happens sometimes when players have very good early experiences at a tougher game. The vagaries of chance work both ways. It feels like you're crushing the game when you're really just getting extremely lucky. Now maybe the law of averages is catching up with you and you are feeling the effects of a game that really is too tough.

I'm not saying you *must* drop down in stakes. But you should at least consider it. There's no shame in moving back down to the calm waters of a game filled with easy opponents. Build up your bankroll again and take another stab at the tougher game later. Unless you're a proposition player hired by the poker room to keep games going, you are completely free to play wherever and whenever you want. Don't let your ego get in the way of taking advantage of the softest games in the room – even if you might think they're beneath you.

Avoid Denial: Don't Make Excuses for Losing

Hang around poker rooms long enough and you will be convinced that everyone is a skillful winning player who has just had temporary interruptions of extremely bad luck. Losses are often attributed to matters unrelated to the poor skill of the player.

Over the years I've assembled a list of the great excuses players have for shifting responsibility from their own shoulders for their lack of poker success. They have helped me see how easy it is to fall into the strong current of denial. I hope you'll recognize the same. By looking at the excuses, I hope we'll be able to see the path toward better self awareness.

The Game was so Good I Couldn't Leave

I hear this regularly from a buddy of mine who is a consistent loser. He thinks the game is filled with lousy players. And it may be. But he is among them, as he passively and loosely plays as if he is on autopilot – especially as his session drags on well beyond his ability to play his best game. Remember that a game with bad players is only profitable if you are playing at your best.

I was Down to my Last Few Chips

This is an excuse that came out of the ranks of tournament players who have refused to accept that they still have a chance even if they only have a "chip and a chair". In a cash game they've reached a point of fatalism where losing the rest of their money doesn't matter. And so they spew their remaining $100 or so for no reason at all. You must realize that the last $100 you lose is as valuable as the first $100.

I was Really Tired From a Long Session

This is a great excuse that implies great stamina and courage. In fact, it betrays a lack of will power and self-control. Why play so long that you become exhausted? Why not leave before your play goes downhill? There's no award for playing poorly under terrible circumstances.

I was Bored at the Low Stakes

This is a doubly great excuse in that it implies both that you usually play bigger (and must therefore be a pretty good player) and that you are so good you get bored with the infantile play of the low rollers. Unfortunately for you, it also raises the question of why, if you are such a hotshot, you dropped down in stakes to begin with. It puts a spotlight on your serious flaw of not being able to play skillfully whenever you play.

I was Playing Over my Head

This is a good excuse in that it injects some modesty. It helps the excuse appear more honest and legitimate. The problem is that you don't recognize that you and only you control when and in what game you play. It raises the question of why you entered the tough game to begin with, and why you didn't leave as soon as you realized you were outmatched.

I was Drinking Heavily (or Otherwise Buzzed)

This slickly casts off responsibility for your losses by blaming "evil rum" or some other inanimate villain over which you seemingly have no control. Even as we might be nodding our heads in understanding that alcohol and drug use may be caused by a medical problem beyond our immediate control, it raises the more serious question of why you chose to play poker while under the damaging influence of booze or drugs. You may forever be an alcoholic, but you never have to play when you are drinking.

I was Distracted by Problems at Home

Yes, we are all sympathetic, as we've all had these from time to time. But again, the excuse only carries you as far as the poker table. Once you cross that threshold and put your money down, you raise the question of why you didn't exercise the necessary poker skill of self control by staying away from the felt until you "got your mind right".

I've Just Been Running Bad

This is the most superficial and least creative of the excuses. It really isn't an excuse at all, just a statement of fact. Your losing streak is proof that you have been running bad. The problem that this excuse reveals is the elevation of the losing streak to the level of the inevitable – as if it was and continues to be a matter of fate. It also implies some inevitability going forward, as if there is nothing you can do about it. The opposite is surely true. No losing streak extends one moment into the future. It can only be viewed retrospectively. It has no predictive powers.

Excuses are just ways of distracting you from the important business of seriously looking at your play to determine why it is that you losing. It may simply be the result of variance. But only an honest assessment can determine that – and point you in the right direction going forward.

Going Pro: Should You Consider it?

Just as a long string of losing sessions highlights certain problems the serious player must address, so too does winning raise other concerns. One of those is the question of "turning pro" – becoming a full-time professional poker player. Some players, after experiencing a few weeks or months of successful poker play, imagine that they might have the chops to play poker for a living. It's a seductive thought.

But before you quit your day job, I'd like you to think about a few matters.

Players sometimes walk themselves to the point of considering poker as a career by doing some simple math. They view their records and see that over the past month, playing 40 hours of $1/2 no limit hold'em, they've managed to win $2,000. They realize that 40 hours is about a week's work on their straight job. If they can make $2,000 in 40 hours playing poker, maybe they could quit their job and play poker instead, making $2,000 a week. If they work 50 weeks out of the year – generously giving themselves two weeks off (but who would need time off? You love playing poker and would gladly do it all the time!) they'd earn $100,000 a year – much more than they make now. They also realize that they have earned this $2,000 playing 40 hours of $1/2. If they move up, as people do after they gain a lot of experience, they might be able to beat a bigger game. Instead of winning $2,000 at $1/2, they'd be able to maybe double that to $4,000 a week at $2/5. That would be $200,000 a year – a princely sum. And it's tax free too, making it worth more like $250,000. Plus, with all their play they'd be earning comp points sufficient to feed them. So their imagination goes.

It seems like a wonderful dream just waiting to come true.

But let's just slow things down a bit, and look more closely at the math. I think you'll quickly see that things aren't quite as rosy as they initially appear.

First of all, are your records completely accurate? Some players, eager to demonstrate their prowess, exclude certain results even as they are keeping score. They suffer some horrible bad beat, or they go on tilt, or they take a stab at a really big game, and they give themselves a mulligan, not recording the horrendous session. So their records, well kept as they appear to be, are at least somewhat inflated.

Okay. Maybe you never have done that. Maybe your $2,000 for 40 hours of play is accurate. But it's surely not reflective of what it would be like if you played 40 hours a week as your job.

First of all, your sample size of 40 hours is just way too small. The general wisdom is that you need to play a full 500 hours before you get a real sense of whether or not your winnings are the product of temporary good luck or skill. I don't know why it's 500 hours as opposed to 300 hours or 1,000 hours. But it's a damn site more than just 40 hours. I've known many great players who have suffered horrible losing streaks for months. Surely, 40 hours is way too short to be any indication of your true poker chops.

Similarly, look at the nature of the hours when you played your 40 hours. Unless you are extremely unusual, the 40 hours you played will tend to be at night and on weekends or holidays. Those are exactly when the games tend to be softest, with the most tourists in the game. When you turn poker into your job, you won't necessarily be able to find 40 hours every single week when you're up against drinking, fun-loving tourists. Similarly, you may not be at your best every time you go to play. You're likely to become tired, sick, distracted, uninterested for at least some of the time that you're on the clock.

So your sample size is way too small, and you're cherry picking only the best 10 hours a week in which to play. You're also making a completely invalid assumption about what will happen when you move up. You might find that you can barely earn as much playing $2/5 as you could playing $1/2.

You've made another incorrect assumption when you joyfully exclaimed that you can make this money tax free. In the US at least, you are responsible for paying taxes on all your income, just as if you were working a straight job. The fact that there is no employer to reach in and deduct taxes from your winnings is no excuse. If an audit is done and you are found out, you will have to pay all of your back taxes plus interest and severe penalties for tax evasion. And even if you're not caught, if you declare no income, you will have a very hard time getting a loan for anything – including a mortgage or a car. Good luck with that.

Playing poker for a living is a nice dream. A rare few actually accomplish it. But poker changes when it becomes your job. You rely on it. You must win if you are to survive. That may have a negative impact on your ability to play profitably. You may be less inclined to take any risks. As we have seen, calculated risks are necessary for optimal play. If you are constantly thinking about how you can't afford to lose, because you have bills to pay, you may be torpedoing your best game.

My advice is simple. Don't even think about turning pro until you've got at least 500 hours of profitable play under your belt. Then you can look at when you're playing and when you might play if you went full time. But you've also got to consider having enough in savings to pay your bills and fund your play. You'll need a living account and a playing bankroll account. The rule of thumb is that you want 100 or so maximum buy-ins as your cushion for confident poker play. Similarly, it's generally considered prudent to have half a year of expenses for savings.

To spell it out: If you want to quit your day job and become a full-time professional you'll want two pots of money in the bank to start with. You won't want to have to use your poker bankroll for your living expenses, so you'll want your living expenses already in the bank to draw from. On top of that, you'll want your poker playing bankroll.

How much exactly will you need? A frugal, single person can probably get by on $40,000 a year for living expenses, and it's generally considered prudent to have half of that saved already. So you'll need $20,000 in the bank to live off. In addition, you'll want 100 buy-ins of $300 for the $1/2 game. That's another $30,000.

All totaled, you'll need $50,000 in savings to start your life as a full-time professional poker player.

I suggest to anyone considering this that you keep your straight job – at least some straight job, and work playing poker as a part-time job. Do it for a couple of years and see how you like it. You might cotton to it, and decide to make your part-time job a full-time job. On the other hand, you might just as soon stay as a part-time pro. You'll have the safety net of a straight job, plus the discipline of keeping regular hours. All the while, if you are a student of the game, you should be improving your skills all the while.

Conclusion

For me, poker is a great and profitable hobby. By focusing on the elements of strategy and tactics in this book, and applying them carefully and rigorously, I am confident that you will give yourself an excellent opportunity to win money from the game – even when considering the considerable amount paid to the house in rake. Good luck with your journey.

Glossary of Terms

ABC Player: A conventional, conservative, moderately tight and aggressive player who is also predictable to a fault.

All-in: Having used all of one's chips to call a bet or a raise. The act of putting in all of one's chips into the pot.

Ante: An amount of money each player must put into the pot to start a hand. In hold'em this is usually done only in the latter stages of a tournament.

Back-door straight or flush draw: Having three of the five cards needed to make a flush or a straight on the flop.

Belly-buster straight draw: An inside straight draw.

Bet: A wager. The act of making a wager.

Big ace: Pocket cards consisting of an ace and a premium card, such as A-K or A-Q.

Blind: A forced bet used to initiate action, starting with the player to the left of the dealer.

Blind, big or large: The forced bet from the player two to the left of the dealer, usually equal to twice that of the small blind.

Blind off: To continue to take the blind of an absent or otherwise inactive tournament player until he loses his entire stack.

Blind raise: A raise, usually to the immediate left of the big blind, made before being dealt cards.

Blind, small: The forced bet to the immediate left of the dealer, usually half that of the large blind.

Blind steal: Winning the blinds with a bluff.

Bluff: A bet designed to get other players to fold by representing a strong hand when the player's hand is actually weak. The act of making such a bet.

Board: The exposed cards in play; also known as community cards.

Brush: A casino employee who directs players to tables.

Burn: To discard the top card of the deck prior to dealing the flop, turn, and river.

Burn card: That card that is burned before the flop, tum, and river.

Button: The player who is designated as the dealer for betting purposes. Also the large disc, usually made of plastic, used to make such a designation.

Call: To place into the pot an amount equal to the bet of the immediately prior bettor. Also the amount placed into the pot when making a call.

Calling station: A player who frequently calls and seldom raises.

Cards speak: A poker rule which declares that the best hand wins, regardless of what a player declares his hand to be. Casino games are always played "cards speak."

Check: A declaration by a player that he chooses not to initiate the betting in any betting round. Also the act of making a check.

Check-raise: To check with the intention of raising after someone else bets. The act of making this check and then the subsequent raise.

Check-raise bluff: A check-raise designed to induce an opponent to fold by representing a weak hand as a strong hand.

Check-raise semi-bluff: A checkraise designed to induce an opponent to fold by representing a strong hand when the player has a weaker hand but could improve to a stronger hand on the next card dealt. The act of making such a check-raise.

Community cards: The exposed cards in the middle of the table that may be used by all players to make the best five-card hand. Also known as the board.

Dealer: Both the person who is dealing the cards and the player who is designated to receive cards last. The player who is designated as dealer also bets last, except on the pre-flop betting round.

Dealer's choice: A type of poker game where each player may declare which poker game is being played, either for his deal or for some predetermined number of hands.

Deep: The amount of chips one has, usually referred to in general terms. Sizing up an opponent, to determine how much an all-in bet might be, a player might ask: "How deep are you?"

Double-belly buster: A straight draw that consists of two ways to hit an inside straight draw. Having the 7♥-9♦ with a board of 5♦-8♥-J♠ is an example of a double belly-buster.

Down card: A card dealt to a player that remains unexposed until the showdown.

Drawing dead: To be so far behind another player that, even if you catch the hand you are drawing for, you will still be behind. For example, if your opponent has a full house on the turn and you are drawing for a flush, you are drawing dead.

Drop: A rake taken from the pot, usually at the beginning of the betting, instead of at the end.

Early position: Early position means those who must act sooner rather than later in any round of poker.

Effective stack: The amount of money or chips that can still be bet in a hand. For example, if only two players are remain in the pot and one player has $100 remaining and the other $50 then the effective stack is $50.

Fast: Game conditions with a lot of aggressive play. Similarly, a type of player who tends to frequently raise and re-raise.

Fixed-limit: Stakes which are limited to a specific amount on each betting round. For example, a fixed-limit $10/$20 game would allow for only $10 bets or raises initially and on the flop, and only $20 bets on the turn and river.

Floor person: A casino employee who helps settle disputes and otherwise keeps the game running smoothly.

Flop: The first three exposed cards in hold'em, dealt at the same time. Also the second round of betting in hold'em.

Fold: To decline to participate further in the hand, typically done when faced with a bet which a player declines to call. The act of making a fold.

Forced bet: A mandatory bet. The small and large blinds are forced bets.

Gutshot: An inside straight draw. Also known as a "belly buster."

Hold'em, Texas hold'em: A popular casino poker game where each player gets two down cards, with five community cards dealt face up. The player's hand is the best combination of the community cards and the down cards.

Implied odds: The odds that the pot will eventually offer you if you make all of the expected bets and your opponents make all of their expected bets.

Juice: The rake, or time charge that the house takes from the players or out of the pot. The vigorish.

Kicker: A high card that distinguishes between two players with the same pair, same two pair, same trips, or same four of a kind.

Late position: Late in the betting order of a hand.

Live blind: A blind that retains the ability to raise if other players merely call and don't raise his blind. The small blind and big blind are live blinds.

Loose: A style of play typified by a lot of calling.

Maniac: A loose player who also plays very aggressively.

Maximum rake: The most the house may rake from a pot. Typically, this is expressed after the percentage of the pot that the house takes. For example, a 10% $4 maximum rake means that the house takes 10% of the pot up to a maximum of $4 a hand.

Middle position: Not early or late betting position.

Mississippi Straddle: A straddle that may be made from any position except the natural blinds, with preference given to the player on the button.

No-limit: A game other than fixed-limit or pot-limit. A no-limit game, played table stakes, would allow each player to bet all of the money he has in front of him at any time.

Online: On the Internet.

Over-the-top: A re-raise.

Pocket, as in "pocket aces": Concealed cards. The two starting cards in hold'em.

Pot: The amount of money in the center of a poker table which is awarded to the winning hand.

Pot-limit: A type of poker in which bets and raises may not exceed the size of the pot.

Pot odds: The odds the pot is offering you for calling a bet.

Pre-flop: The first betting round, before the flop has been dealt.

Protected pot: A pot with more than two remaining players, especially on the last round of betting.

Raise: An action by a player that increases the size of the bet. The amount of money used in this action.

Rake: The amount taken out of the pot by the house. Also the act of taking this amount out of the pot.

Re-raise: A raise after another player has already raised. The act of making a raise of a raise.

River: The final betting round in hold'em, when the fifth and final community card is exposed.

Rock: A very tight player.

Round: Each betting interval, after which another card is dealt or the final showdown of the hand takes place.

Semi-bluff: A bluff which has some expectation of improving into the best hand on the next card dealt.

Semi-demi-bluff: A bet which may be representing the strongest hand, may win the pot as a bluff, and which may improve into the best hand on the next card dealt.

Showdown: That moment after the last bet is called when players expose their cards and see who has the best hand to win the pot.

Side pot: The pot established after a player is all-in. The side pot will be won by one of the players remaining in the betting, and not by the all-in player.

Sit and go: A type of one-table tournament that begins when there is a table full of players ready to play. It is characterized by quickly rising blinds and a relatively short stack to begin, favoring aggressive play.

Slowplay: To deliberately not bet or raise in order to represent a weaker hand than one actually has.

Steaming: To be on tilt. To play aggressively and erratically, giving in to emotions rather than using logic while playing.

Stack (or stack size): The amount of money or chips a player has on the table.

Straddle: A voluntary blind bet usually made to the immediate left of the large blind that is usually twice as large as the large blind. It is live.

String bet: A bet where someone moves chips into the pot in more than one motion. String bets are not allowed in a casino.

String raise: A raise made in two motions, where someone moves chips in to the pot to call the bet and then returns to his stack and makes a second motion to raise the pot. String raises are not allowed in a casino.

Stud: A type of poker where some of the cards dealt to each player are dealt face up. The typical casino stud game is 7-card stud. Other variations include 5-card stud and razz, which is 7-card stud low.

Sweat: To watch the play of another player, while not actually involved in the hand.

Table stakes: Limiting the stakes which may be bet to those that are in front of the player when the betting round begins.

Tells: Actions, usually unintentional, made by players that may reveal to other players the true strength or weakness of a hand.

Three-bet: A pre-flop re-raise of the player who initially raises the blinds.

Tight: A style of play typified by a lot of folding.

Tilt: A condition whereby a player's betting action is out of control, often typified by a lot of loose calls and inexplicable raises.

Time: An amount paid to the house by every active player in a game every half hour or hour. This is done instead of the house taking a rake, especially in large games.

Tip: An amount of money voluntarily given to a casino employee, generally the dealer, usually when winning a pot.

Toke: A tip.

Trap: To seduce an opponent into betting or raising when you slowplay a hand you think is very strong. A action of making this play.

Turn: The third round of betting, when the fourth up card is exposed.

Up: Two pair. "Aces up" means two pair, with the Aces as the higher pair. Similarly "Jacks up" means two pair with Jacks as the higher pair.

Up card: A card intentionally dealt face up.

Variance: Essentially the effect of luck on the game of poker. Variance recognizes that a player can play well and lose because luck will "vary".

Weak ace: Pocket cards consisting of an ace and a weak second card, for example A-4 or A-3.

Wild man: A maniac.

X, as in A-x: An unspecified card is denoted by x. For example, A-x means an ace and another card.

7-Card Stud: A game played with each player receiving seven cards, four of which are dealt face up. The hands consist of the best poker hand among five of the seven cards.